STUDY GUIDE TO ACCOMPANY

CRIMINAL LAW & PROCEDURE
AN INTRODUCTION

RONALD J. BACIGAL
UNIVERSITY OF RICHMOND

PREPARED BY

CINDY E. SHEAFFER, ESQUIRE
LEGAL STUDIES DIVISION
CENTRAL PENNSYLVANIA BUSINESS SCHOOL

WEST PUBLISHING COMPANY
MINNEAPOLIS/ST. PAUL   NEW YORK   LOS ANGELES   SAN FRANCISCO

WEST'S COMMITMENT TO THE ENVIRONMENT

In 1906, West Publishing Company began recycling materials left over from the production of books. This began a tradition of efficient and responsible use of resources. Today, 100% of our legal bound volumes are printed on acid-free, recycled paper consisting of 50% new paper pulp and 50% paper that has undergone a de-inking process. We also use vegetable-based inks to print all of our books. West recycles nearly 27,700,000 pounds of scrap paper annually—the equivalent of 229,300 trees. Since the 1960s, West has devised ways to capture and recycle waste inks, solvents, oils, and vapors created in the printing process. We also recycle plastics of all kinds, wood, glass, corrugated cardboard, and batteries, and have eliminated the use of polystyrene book packaging. We at West are proud of the longevity and the scope of our commitment to the environment.

West pocket parts and advance sheets are printed on recyclable paper and can be collected and recycled with newspapers. Staples do not have to be removed. Bound volumes can be recycled after removing the cover.

Production, Prepress, Printing and Binding by West Publishing Company.

TEXT IS PRINTED ON 10% POST CONSUMER RECYCLED PAPER

Printed with Printwise
Environmentally Advanced Water Washable Ink

610 Opperman Drive
P.O. Box 64526
St. Paul, MN 55164–0526

Printed in the United States of America
03 02 01 00 99 98 97 96 8 7 6 5 4 3 2 1 0

ISBN 0–314–06965–8

TABLE OF CONTENTS

CHAPTER 1

DEFINING AND PROVING CRIMES

The purpose of criminal law is to punish those members of society who violate our criminal laws, which have been designed to benefit all of society. Within our system, the government is the only entity that can use physical force (death penalty and imprisonment) to coerce people into behaving as society wants them to behave.

This chapter discusses the different forms of punishment, the sources of our laws, and the criminal trial. After reviewing this chapter, some of the differences between criminal law and civil law will become more clear.

OUTLINE

I. Purposes of Criminal Law

A. The purpose of criminal law differs from that of civil law - in criminal law, the purpose is to punish the wrongdoer; in civil law, the purpose is to compensate the victim

B. Forms of Punishment

1. **Incapacitation/Restraint** - restraining criminals in prison or executing criminals so they cannot commit crimes in the future

2. **Specific Deterrence** - punishing a criminal to deter that person from committing future crimes

3. **General Deterrence** - punishing a criminal to deter the public from committing crimes

4. **Rehabilitation** - forcing a criminal to undergo some form of social education to prevent future crime

5. **Retribution** - vindicating a wrong - the public relies on the legal system to vindicate wrongs, which lessens the desire for private revenge

II. Sources of Criminal Law

A. **Common Law** - judge-made law which defines crimes and establishes the rules of criminal responsibility according to custom and tradition

1. **Judicial Activism** - judges interpret the law to achieve broad social goals

2. **Judicial Restraint** - judges view judicial power as strictly limited by the separation of powers doctrine and by earlier case decisions

B. **Model Penal Code** - a suggested model for enactment and interpretation of criminal law - the Model Penal Code is not the law unless adopted and enacted by a legislature

C. **Statutory Law** - criminal codes passed by the legislature which define crimes

1. **Legislative Intent** - the purpose for which the legislators enacted a particular statute

D. **Administrative Regulations** - regulations promulgated by administrative agencies which identify certain conduct as criminal

1. **Vagueness Doctrine** - holds that any administrative regulation or statute is unconstitutional when citizens "must necessarily guess at its meaning and differ as to its application"

E. **Constitutional Limitations** - certain provisions of the U. S. Constitution limit the legislative power to create crimes, guarantee procedural fairness to criminal defendants, or limit the government's power to prohibit and punish certain conduct

1. **Bills of Attainder** - legislative acts convicting an individual of a crime

2. **Ex Post Facto Laws** - laws that retroactively make innocent conduct illegal, increase the punishment for a criminal act, or decrease the standard of proof required for a conviction

III. Proving the Crime

A. Criminal Trial

1. The prosecution must prove that a defined crime occurred and that the defendant committed the crime

2. The prosecution presents evidence, then the defendant presents evidence, and then the factfinder (jury or judge) decides whose presentation of facts is legally persuasive

   a. In a jury trial, the jury determines the facts and the judge determines the law

   b. In a bench trial, the judge determines the facts and the law

3. Burden of Proof - a criminal defendant is presumed to be innocent

   a. The prosecution bears the burden of proving beyond a reasonable doubt all facts necessary to constitute the crime

      i. **Proof Beyond a Reasonable Doubt** - proof that excludes every reasonable hypothesis except guilt, proof that excludes every reasonable possibility of innocence, or proof to a moral certainty

   b. **Corpus Delicti** - the body of the crime - the fact that a crime has been committed

   c. **Directed Verdict of Acquittal** - the trial judge may enter an acquittal whenever a rational jury must conclude that the prosecution failed to prove guilt beyond a reasonable doubt

   d. **Ultimate Issue** - the question of whether the defendant is guilty or not guilty of the crime

   e. **Affirmative Defense** - the defendant admits committing the acts charged, but seeks to justify or excuse his or her conduct by establishing additional facts

   f. **Preponderance of the Evidence** - the standard of proof usually required to establish an affirmative defense; asks the jury to determine whether more likely than not (more than 50%) the facts support the affirmative defense

4. Presumptions and Permissible Inferences

   1. **Presumption** - a fact that must be inferred (presumed) on the basis of certain predicate facts that have been proved

   2. **Permissive Inference** - a possible conclusion that may be drawn but is not exclusively required if certain predicate facts are proved

KEY TERMS

common law
judicial activism
judicial restraint
Model Penal Code
legislative intent
vagueness doctrine
bills of attainder
ex post facto laws
burden of proof
proof beyond a reasonable doubt
corpus delicti
directed verdict of acquittal
ultimate issue
affirmative defense
preponderance of the evidence
presumption
permissive inference

REVIEW QUESTIONS

Fill-in-the-Blank

1. The effectiveness of a general deterrent depends on what factors?

   ____

   ____

2. The ______________________ was promulgated by the American Law Institute, an association of lawyers, judges and legal scholars.

3. ______________________ is the purpose particular legislators express during debate over passage of a proposed statute.

4. The Department of Agriculture promulgates ______________________, which supplement the more general laws enacted by Congress.

5. A statute which makes it illegal to behave in an immodest way in public would be an example of a statute which is ____________________________.

6. The highest standard of proof in the law is ____________________________.

7. The fact that a crime has been committed is called the ____________________________ of the crime.

8. A(n) ____________________________ admits that the defendant did the acts charged, but offers additional facts that justifies or excuses the defendant's conduct.

9. A fact that <u>must</u> be inferred on the basis of certain predicate facts that have been proved is called a(n) ____________________________.

10. A(n) ____________________________ is a possible conclusion that <u>may</u> be drawn if certain predicate facts are proven.

<u>Essay</u>

1. Explain the difference between the purpose of civil law and the purpose of criminal law.

2. The death penalty could fall into several different categories of forms of punishment. List two (2) of those categories and explain how the death penalty would control behavior in each instance.

3. After the prosecution and the defendant have presented their evidence in a criminal trial, the judge will instruct the jury on three (3) issues. Explain those three (3) issues.

4. Explain the difference between the standard of beyond a reasonable doubt and by a preponderance of the evidence.

CHAPTER 2

ESSENTIAL ELEMENTS OF CRIME

While criminal law can be categorized in different ways (punishment, mental state and harm), crimes are defined by society's conceptions of three basic elements: mental state, physical act, and social harm. Combining these three elements gives us the "working definition of crime." This definition can be used to determine the legal requirements of any crime.

Many technical terms are used in the field of criminal law when describing conduct that is prohibited; however, these concepts are all based in a foundation of the three elements of the working definition. This chapter looks at each of these elements in depth, and shows how they come together to define crime.

<u>OUTLINE</u>

I. Elements of Working Definition of Crime

A. Social Harm

1. Society classifies what is considered to be a social harm; it is not created by lawyers and judges based on their own perceptions

2. Social harm encompasses harm to all of society rather than harm to one member (civil law). In criminal law, the case is brought by the State or the United States rather than by an individual

3. Social harm can change from jurisdiction to jurisdiction and from time period to time period

B. Physical Act

1. A physical can be a deliberate body movement OR an omission or failure to act when the law imposes a duty to act

2. Categories of affirmative physical acts:

   a. **Evil Thought** - when one makes a decision in private thought to commit a crime - society does not punish people for their evil thoughts, only for their conduct

   b. **Express Thought** - when one verbalizes an evil thought to another - punishment of express thoughts conflicts with the right to freedom of speech - in most cases, a physical act beyond a mere verbal statement is required for a crime; however, in some instances, the mere utterance of words can be a crime, i.e., perjury

   c. **Request** - when one asks another to join in a criminal plan - the crime of solicitation is complete when the request is made

   d. **Agreement** - when two or more persons agree that they will jointly commit a crime - this is sufficient for crime of conspiracy - most statutes require an overt act in furtherance of the conspiracy to complete the crime of conspiracy

   e. **Attempt** requires an overt act (a substantial step toward the commission of the crime) for an attempted crime

   f. **Consummation** is when one commits all the physical acts required of the crime

C. Mental State (Mens Rea)

   a. **Specific Intent** is a subjective desire or intent to bring about a social harm (premeditation, malice aforethought for criminal homicide) - this is the most blameworthy category

   b. **Wanton State of Mind** is an extreme reckless disregard of the safety of others - this is the second most blameworthy category

   c. **Willful State of Mind** is the actual knowledge of the threat to another's safety - this, along with wanton state of mind, is the second most blameworthy category

   d. **Negligence** is when one fails to act as a reasonably prudent person under the circumstances (civil, noncriminal)

e. **Recklessness**, or criminal negligence, is a gross deviation from a law-abiding person's conduct - this is the third most blameworthy category

f. **Strict liability crimes** are when one commits an act that causes a prohibited harm, regardless of his state of mind or reasonableness of actions - strict liability crimes are always created by statute

II. Causation

A. **Factual Cause** ("but-for test of causation")

1. To determine factual cause, ask "but for" the person's act, would the social harm have occurred

2. Apply objective scientific principles of cause and effect

3. This is a starting point, it does not tell us whether to punish this person

B. **Legal Cause**

1. The legal cause is the assessment of the social purposes to be served by the criminal law

C. Criminal law requires you find a person's actions have been both the factual cause and the legal cause of the social harm

KEY TERMS

mens rea
actus rea
deliberate bodily movement
omission
overt act for a conspiracy
overt act for an attempted crime
mere preparation
specific intent
wanton state of mind
willful state of mind
reasonably prudent person standard
negligence
recklessness (criminal negligence)
strict liability crimes
factual cause
legal causation

REVIEW QUESTIONS

Fill-in-the-Blank

1. The three elements of the "working definition of crime" are ____________________, ____________________, and ____________________.

2. The two fundamental principles that underlie the criminal law's requirement for a physical act are ____________________ and ____________________.

3. The crime of ____________________ has been committed when one person requests that another person join in a plan to commit a crime.

4. The crime of ____________________ has been committed when two or more persons agree to a plan to commit a crime and then take a step in furtherance of the agreement.

5. When the defendant subjectively intends or desires to bring about the prohibited social harm, the mens rea is called ____________________.

6. A ____________________ state of mind is an extremely reckless disregard for the safety of others; a ____________________ state of mind is an actual knowledge of the threat to another's safety.

7. The ____________________ standard measures the defendant's actual conduct against that of a ____________________ under the same or similar circumstances.

8. ____________________ crimes occur when the defendant commits an act that causes a prohibited harm, regardless of the defendant's state of mind or reasonableness of actions.

Essay

1. Explain how harm is classified differently in criminal law than in civil law.

2. Peter Jones is watching a detective story on television in which a man commits a burglary of a convenience. The man is eventually caught and punished. Peter decides that he could commit the same crime, only not make the same mistakes, and therefore not get caught. He stays up all night thinking about how to carry out his plan. Has Peter committed a crime? Why or why not?

3. Explain the difference between negligence (noncriminal) and recklessness (criminal negligence).

4. Explain the difference between a factual cause and a legal cause. Try to come up with an example of a situation where a person's actions were the factual cause but not the legal cause of the harm.

CHAPTER 3

PARTIES TO A CRIME AND INCHOATE OFFENSES

Along with the person who actually commits a crime (the perpetrator), there are other parties that may also be held criminally liable for that crime. This chapter will examine these different parties and their respective criminal responsibility.

Also included in this chapter is a discussion of inchoate, or incomplete, criminal offenses. This chapter uses the three elements of the working definition of crime in order to analyze the different offenses.

OUTLINE

I. Parties to a Crime

A. **Perpetrator** (principal in the first degree) - one who:

1. Performs the physical acts that constitute the crime, or

2. Commits the crime by use of an instrumentality

a. **Instrumentality** - use of an inanimate object, animal, or innocent human being to commit a crime

b. **Innocent Human Agent** - one who commits the physical acts constituting a crime, but who is innocent of the crime because of a legitimate defense

B. **Aider and Abettor** (principal in the second degree) - one who assists the perpetrator in the commission of the crime while being actually or constructively present

C. **Accessory Before the Fact** - one who:

1. Is not present when the crime is committed, and

2. Previously solicited, counseled, or advised another how to commit the crime

D. Similarities between Aiders and Abettors and Accessories Before the Fact (Accomplices)

1. Both are punished only when they perform an affirmative act which assists the perpetrator

2. For both, the defendant must have the mental state required for the crime

3. Both are charged, tried, convicted and punished (except for the death penalty) as if they were perpetrators

4. Both can be held responsible for unintended crimes

E. **Accessory After the Fact**

1. Does not contribute to the commission of the crime

2. Impedes the apprehension, trial, or punishment of a felon

3. To convict the defendant, the prosecution must prove:

   a. A felony was committed;

   b. That defendant knew that the underlying felony had been committed;

   c. That the defendant intended to hinder apprehension, trial or punishment; and

   d. That the defendant assisted the felon to avoid apprehension, trial or punishment

4. An accessory after the fact is not guilty of the committed offense, but may be guilty of a separate crime

   a. **Misprison of a Felony** - failure to report a known crime

   b. **Compounding a Felony** - accepting a benefit in return for concealing a known crime

II. **Inchoate Crimes** - incomplete or imperfect offenses

A. **Solicitation** - when a person invites or requests another to commit a crime

1. Mental State: Defendant specifically intends the other person to commit an offense

2. Physical Act: Defendant requested or invited another to commit an offense - no physical act in furtherance of the crime need be performed by either person

3. Social Harm: Defendant has tempted a presumably innocent person to commit a crime

4. **Merger** - a previously distinct offense is included within a greater offense - defendant can be convicted of either, but not both, offenses

B. **Attempt** - when a person intends to commit a specific offense and then performs an act that constitutes a substantial step toward completing that offense

1. Requires that the specific intent to commit a particular offense is formed in the mind of the defendant

2. **Mere Preparation** - portion of an attempted crime prior to the point at which consummation of the offense begins

3. Tests to determine criminal intent:

a. **Last Proximate Act Test** - Defendant is guilty of an attempt after doing all that he or she believes is necessary to complete the intended crime

b. **Dangerous Proximity Test**

i. Temporal and geographical nearness of the prohibited harm

ii. Seriousness of the harm

iii. Degree of apprehension created

c. **Probable Desistance Test** - focuses on how far the defendant has proceeded and the likelihood that the defendant will persist in the planned crime

C. **Impossibility**

1. **Factual Impossibility** - a claim of defense because the defendant's conduct could not succeed in bringing about the intended offense

2. **Legal Impossibility** - a claim of defense because the defendant's state of mind precludes commission of a recognized crime

D. **Abandonment**

1. Discontinuation of a plan to commit a crime

2. Sometimes recognized as a valid defense to charges of attempting to commit the crime

E. **Conspiracy** - an agreement by two or more persons to commit an unlawful act

1. Mental State: two or more persons form a specific intent to accomplish an unlawful act

2. Physical Act: commission of an overt act in furtherance of the conspiracy

3. Social Harm: two or more people who unite to commit a crime is a more dangerous situation than one person acting alone

4. **Wheel Conspiracies** - center of the wheel is one person (hub) who has contact with other persons (spokes)

a. No direct contact is necessary between every member

b. Some community of interest must be shown

5. **Chain Conspiracies** - parties are linked together in linear fashion - courts look to:

a. Community of interest among the parties

b. Each link in the chain relied upon other links to complete their tasks

6. **Wharton's Rule** - no conspiracy can occur in an agreement between only the parties necessary for the commission of a substantive offense

7. Liability of Coconspirators

a. Some jurisdictions punish for the completed crime and for the conspiracy to commit the crime

b. Some jurisdictions merge conspiracy offenses into the completed crimes

c. **Pinkerton Doctrine** - each member of a conspiracy is criminally responsible for any crime committed by another party to the agreement if it was the object of the conspiracy or a natural consequence of the unlawful agreement

KEY TERMS

perpetrator (principal in the first degree)
instrumentality
innocent human agent
aider and abettor (principal in the second degree)
accessory before the fact
accessory after the fact
misprison of a felony
compounding a felony
merger
inchoate crimes
solicitation
attempted crimes
mere preparation
factual impossibility
legal impossibility
abandonment
conspiracy
Pinkerton Doctrine
Wharton's Rule

REVIEW QUESTIONS

Fill-in-the-Blank

1. A(n) ________________________ performs the physical acts constituting a crime or uses an instrumentality.

2. The driver of a getaway car is called a(n) ________________________.

3. If John sees Bill commit a crime and then Bill pays John $500 not to tell the police, John is guilty of ________________________.

4. ________________________ is when a previously distinct offense is included within a greater offense.

5. According to People v. Rizzo, ________________________ to commit a crime is not yet an attempted crime.

6. The test to determine criminal intent which focuses on how far the defendant has proceeded and the likelihood that he or she will persist in the planned crime is called the ________________________ test.

7. If a person discontinues his plan to commit a crime, it is called ________________________.

8. The crime of bribery requires at least two persons. According to ________________________, no conspiracy can occur between only those two persons involved in the bribery.

9. The ________________________ places criminal liability on each member of a conspiracy for criminal acts committed by other members.

10. In addition to possessing the requisite mental state, a person must commit a(n) ________________________ act to be guilty of conspiracy.

Essay

1. Explain the difference between factual impossibility and legal impossibility and give an example of each.

2. Bonnie approaches Clyde and asks him to assist her in robbing a bank. Clyde refuses. Has a crime been committed by Bonnie? By Clyde? If so, explain what crime.

3. A and B decide to rob a 7-Eleven store. The plan is that A will take a loaded gun into the store and hold up the clerk. B is the driver and he will stay in the car and wait for A to come out with the money, and then they'll drive away. Both A and B agree that A will only use the gun to frighten the clerk, not to fire it at anyone. A goes into the 7-Eleven and when the clerk sees the gun, he activates

the alarm system. A panics and shoots and kills the clerk. Does B have any criminal liability for the clerk's death? If so, explain what it is.

4. Explain the social harm that exists with a conspiracy to commit a crime.

CHAPTER 4

DEFENSES

When a defendant raises a defense to a crime he is charged with, he is admitting he performed the act charged, but he is raising a specific excuse or justification to which the prosecution must respond. There are two general categories into which defenses fall: a case-in-chief defense and an affirmative defense. This chapter distinguishes between those two classifications of defenses, and then it examines the different defenses that may be raised by a defendant, as well as the burden of proof required at the time of trial regarding these defenses.

OUTLINE

I. **Case-in-Chief Defenses** - challenge the prosecution's version of the facts, but do not introduce an independent legal claim into the case

  A. **Alibi** - a claim that the defendant was not in a position to commit the crime charged

II. **Affirmative Defenses** - the defendant admits committing the acts charged, but seeks to justify or excuse the defendant's conduct by establishing additional facts

III. Defenses

  A. Compulsion, Necessity, and Duress (affirmative defenses)

    1. **Compulsion** - general concept wherein defendant claims he was compelled to violate the law in order to accomplish some greater good or to avoid a greater evil

    2. **Necessity** - excuses a violation of criminal law if:

      a. The defendant reasonably believed the threat of harm was imminent;

      b. The only way to prevent the threatened harm was to violate the law; and

c. The harm that was caused by violating the law is less serious than the harm the defendant sought to avoid

3. **Duress** - an unlawful threat of imminent death or serious bodily injury, which induces a person to commit a crime; may be used as a defense except in the case of murder

B. Mistake as a Defense (case-in-chief defense)

1. **Mistake of Fact** - a lack of knowledge of a particular piece of information which may be a defense if it negates a material element of the offense

2. **Mistake of Law** - a lack of knowledge of a particular law which may be a defense if it negates the mens rea required for the crime

C. Intoxication - caused either by drugs or alcohol

1. **Voluntary Intoxication** (case-in-chief defense) - may be a defense if it produces clouded mental facilities that negate the mental state required for a particular crime

2. **Involuntary Intoxication** (case-in-chief or affirmative defense) - may be a defense if the defendant did not know of the ingested substances's intoxicating effect or if someone forced or tricked the defendant into ingesting the intoxicating substance

D. Insanity (case-in-chief or affirmative defense) - can arise at different stages of criminal proceedings

1. **Competency to Stand Trial** - the defendant must be rational, possess the ability to testify coherently, and be able to meaningfully discuss the case with defense counsel

2. **Mental Illness at the Time of Punishment**

a. Eighth Amendment (cruel and unusual punishment clause) prohibits execution of a person who has become insane after being sentenced to death

b. Persons may be transferred to medical facilities within or outside the penitentiary or may be forced to accept antipsychotic medication

3. **Insanity as a Defense**

   a. May be a complete defense to all charges

   b. Definitions change from jurisdiction to jurisdiction

   c. Legal tests for insanity:

      i. **M'Naghten Test** - determines whether the defendant is able to distinguish right from wrong

      ii. **Irresistible Impulse Test** - determines whether the defendant acted from an uncontrollable impulse

      iii. **Diminished Capacity Test** - recognizes that defendants may lack "substantial" but not total mental capacity

      iv. **Federal Test** - uses the M'Naghten right-from-wrong standard, but requires that the defendant prove insanity by clear and convincing evidence

E. Justifiable Use of Force

1. Some jurisdictions require the defendant to prove by a preponderance of evidence that the use of force was permissible

2. Some jurisdictions require the prosecution to disprove the justification or excuse once it has been raised by the defendant

3. **Self-Defense** (case-in-chief or affirmative defense) - actions in a situation in which:

   a. The defendant was not the aggressor;

   b. The defendant reasonably perceived an immediate threat of bodily harm;

   c. The defendant reasonably believed that defensive force was necessary to avoid the harm; and

   d. The amount of defensive force used was reasonable

   e. **Retreat** - an avenue of safe escape; a prerequisite to self-defense in some jurisdictions

4. **Defense of Others** (affirmative defense) - the act protecting another from harm, which may excuse or justify the defendant's use of force

   a. **Alter-Ego Theory** - a defendant acts to protect a person who has a lawful right of self-defense

   b. **Reasonable Perception Theory** - the defendant acts upon a perception that the aided person has a right to use defensive force, even when the perception is erroneous

5. **Defense of Property and Habitation** (affirmative defense)

   a. The law places a higher value on life than on property

   b. Defendants are prohibited from using deadly force to protect property

6. **Forcible Arrest and Force Used to Resist Arrest**

   a. An arresting police officer may use only "reasonable" force to apprehend a suspect

   b. Deadly force is constitutionally permissible only when an arresting officer reasonable believes that a suspected felon poses a threat of serious physical, either to the police officer or to others

   c. Most jurisdictions prohibit any resistance to an arrest by a law enforcement officer

   d. A citizen may use defensive force against anyone, including a police officer, who improperly threatens the citizen's life

F. **Entrapment** (affirmative defense)

1. Focuses on whether the defendant was induced to commit the crime by a government agent, usually an undercover police officer and whether the defendant would have committed the offense without the inducement

2. **Subjective Approach** - prohibits police officers from instigating criminal acts by people not predisposed to commit the crime

3. **Objective Approach** - focuses on whether the government's conduct in inducing the crime was beyond judicial toleration

KEY TERMS

Affirmative Defense
Alibi
Alter-Ego Theory of Self-Defense
Case-in-Chief Defense
Competency to Stand Trial
Defense of Others
Diminished Capacity Test for Insanity
Duress
Federal Test for Insanity
Involuntary Intoxication
Irresistible Impulse Test for Insanity
Mistake of Fact
Mistake of Law
M'Naghten Test for Insanity
Necessity
Objective Approach to Entrapment
Reasonable Perception Theory of Self-Defense
Retreat
Self-Defense
Subjective Approach to Entrapment
Voluntary Intoxication

REVIEW QUESTIONS

Fill-in-the-Blank

1. The defense of ________________________ is an unlawful threat of imminent death or serious bodily injury which induces a person to commit a crime.

2. If a defendant claims that he was not in Pittsburgh, the scene of the crime for which he is accused, but was in Seattle at the time the crime was committed, he has a(n) ________________________.

3. The ________________________ test for insanity focuses on whether the defendant acted from an uncontrollable impulse.

4. If Kevin thinks it is legal to smoke marijuana for medical purposes, when in fact it is illegal, this would be an example of a mistake of ________________________.

5. One can never use deadly force to protect ________________________.

6. Janet slips some alcohol into Bob's soda without Bob's knowledge. Bob drinks the soda and later commits a crime. Bob may claim ________________________ as a defense to the crime.

7. The ________________________ theory of self-defense requires that the defendant stand in the shoes of the person she was defending and allows the defendant to use the same force that person would be able to use in defending himself.

8. ________________________ is an avenue of safe escape, and is a prerequisite to self-defense in some jurisdictions.

Essay

1. Explain why the Court in *United States v. Calley* found that Lieutenant Calley had the mens rea for murder.

2. List and explain the elements of the defense of necessity.

3. Explain the difference between a mistake of fact and a mistake of law and give an example of each.

4. Explain the difference between an objective approach to entrapment and a subjective approach to entrapment, and give an example of each.

CHAPTER 5

CRIMES AGAINST A PERSON

This chapter focuses on crimes that are committed against an individual person, beginning with the most serious: criminal homicide. To distinguish which specific type of criminal homicide has been committed, the courts will look to the intent of the defendant. This becomes very important when distinguishing between murder and manslaughter.

Of a less serious nature are the crimes of assault and battery. This chapter discusses the various types of assault and ends by reviewing robbery, violent sex crimes, and kidnapping and false imprisonment.

OUTLINE

I. **Criminal Homicide** - taking another's life in a manner proscribed by law - a killing in the absence of justification or excuse

   A. **Murder** - an unlawful killing with malice aforethought

      1. **Malice Aforethought** - distinguishes murder from manslaughter - occurs when the defendant:

         a. Forms an intent to kill;

         b. Forms an intent to inflict grievous bodily harm on another;

         c. Displays a wanton or extremely reckless disregard for the risk to human life; or

         d. Commits a dangerous felony during the commission of which a death results

      2. **Capital Murder** - a killing characterized by the existence of a statutorily defined aggravating circumstance in addition to the other requirements for murder

3. **First Degree Murder** - a killing characterized by premeditation

   a. **Premeditation** - careful, prior deliberation of an act committed in cold blood

   b. **Instantaneous Premeditation** - a view of forethought to the crime that recognizes that "no time is too short for a wicked man to frame in his mind the scheme of murder"

   c. **Transferred Intent** - the act of killing a person while intending to kill someone else

   d. **Felony-Murder Rule** - applies a first degree murder charge to killing a person intentionally, recklessly, or even accidentally while committing a dangerous felony

4. **Second Degree Murder** - a killing with a state of mind characterized as a wanton or an extreme reckless disregard for the risk to human life

B. **Manslaughter** - an unlawful killing without malice aforethought

1. **Voluntary Manslaughter**

   a. Killing while in a **state of passion** (factual determination for factfinder to make)

   b. Which was caused by **adequate provocation** (circumstances that "would naturally tend to arouse the passion of an ordinarily reasonable person") and

   c. Without a reasonable opportunity to cool off before killing

2. **Involuntary Manslaughter** - a homicide that results from the defendant's reckless or criminally negligent conduct or the defendant's commission of an unlawful act

   a. **Reckless Conduct** - less serious than extreme recklessness but more serious than simple negligence resulting in civil liability - courts consider both the defendant's subjective state of mind and objective evidence of the extent to which the defendant's conduct endangered another

b. **Misdemeanor-Manslaughter** - applies a manslaughter charge to a homicide that results from the defendant's commission of an unlawful act

II. **Assault and Battery** - some jurisdictions have merged assault and battery into a single offense

A. **Battery** - the unlawful application of force to the person of another (unlawful touching)

1. A person cannot consent to any type of conduct that involves serious injury

2. Unlawful touching may involve direct body-to-body contact or an indirect touching by some instrumentality used by the defendant

3. Mental state - either an intent to strike another or a reckless act which results in a touching

B. **Assault**

1. Occurs only if the defendant accompanies a threat with some additional physical conduct

2. Two categories of assault:

a. **Attempted Battery Form of Assault** - act in which the defendant specifically intends to, and comes close to, touching another

b. **Offer Type of Assault** - places another in fear of an imminent battery

3. State of mind - defendant either intends to frighten the victim or recklessly cause the victim to apprehend an imminent touching

C. **Aggravated Assault and Battery** - attacks that result in more serious injuries or create the potential for serious injury because the attacker used a deadly weapon

1. **Mayhem** - a common law crime in which the victim was dismembered or disfigured in such a way that the victim was less able to engage in self-defense

2. **Malicious Wounding** - the shooting, stabbing, cutting, or wounding of any person with the intent to maim, disfigure, disable, or kill

D. **Robbery** - larceny from the victim's person or presence, by use of either force or threats of force

E. **Extortion or Blackmail** - threats to injure a person's reputation or to expose a person to shame and ridicule

III. Violent Sex Crimes

A. **Rape** - at common law, sexual intercourse with a woman other than the defendant's wife by force and without the victim's consent

1. Most statutes today have made the crime of rape gender neutral

2. **Marital Rape Exception** - at common law, a man could not be convicted of raping his wife

a. Based on the theory that a wife was chattel and when she married her husband, she gave continuing consent to sex with him

b. Most jurisdictions today, even those that retain the marital rape exception, recognize that a man who physically forces his wife to have sex with him is guilty of some form of assault and battery

3. **Rape Shield Laws** - laws which prohibit the use of evidence of a victim's prior sexual conduct, except for prior consensual sexual relations with the defendant

IV. Kidnapping and False Imprisonment

A. **Kidnapping** - seizing and carrying away another person by force, threat of force, fraud, or deception (aggravated form of false imprisonment)

1. If the victim is not returned within 24 hours after the taking, it is presumed that the victim was transported across state lines, which makes it a federal offense

2. The carrying away of the victim requires that the forced movement be more than the movement incidental to the commission of another crime

B. **False Imprisonment** - confining a person against the person's will

KEY TERMS

Adequate Provocation
Attempted Battery Form of Assault
Battery
Blackmail
Capital Murder
Common Law Rape
Criminal Homicide
Extortion
False Imprisonment
Felony-Murder Rule
First Degree Murder
Instantaneous Premeditation
Involuntary Manslaughter
Kidnapping
Malice Aforethought
Malicious Wounding
Mayhem
Misdemeanor-Manslaughter
Offer Type of Assault
Premeditation
Rape Shield Law
Robbery
Second Degree Murder
Transferred Intent
Voluntary Manslaughter
Wanton Conduct

REVIEW QUESTIONS

Fill-in-the-Blank

1. ______________________ distinguishes murder from manslaughter.

2. First degree murder is a killing which is characterized by ______________________.

3. The Court in *People v. Stamp* used the ______________________ rule to find the defendant guilty of first degree murder.

4. ______________________ places another in fear of an imminent battery.

5. The crime of ______________________ occurs when the defendant shoots, stabs, cuts or wounds any person with the intent to maim, disfigure, disable, or kill.

6. The use of evidence of the prior sexual conduct of the victim of a rape, except for prior consensual sexual relations with the defendant, is prohibited by ______________________ laws.

7. ________________________ is an aggravated form of false imprisonment.

8. Larceny from the victim's person or presence by the use of either force or the threat of force is called ________________________.

Essay

1. Define malice aforethought and explain how it distinguishes murder from manslaughter.

2. Describe some of the factors that the court may look to when determining whether a killing was premeditated.

3. Explain the difference between voluntary and involuntary manslaughter and give an example of each.

4. Explain the marital rape exception, and explain how this exception originated.

CHAPTER 6

CRIMES AGAINST PROPERTY AND HABITATION

This chapter looks at crimes against property and habitation. Many of these common law definitions have been retained and upheld in modern day statutes, while some of the definitions have been altered and updated. This chapter looks to the elements of each of the crimes and the mental state required for the defendant to be convicted.

OUTLINE

I. Thefts of Private Property

A. **Larceny** - common law elements:

1. Trespassory Taking

a. **Trespass** - taking possession of another's personal property without consent or legal justification

b. **Custody** - physical control of property, but the use of the property is limited by another's lawful possession of the property

c. **Possession** - the right to use property in a reasonably unrestricted manner

2. Carrying Away

a. **Asportation** - any physical movement of property taken from another's possession

b. **Dominion** - carrying away from another's possession into the defendant's control

3. Personal Property - excludes real estate and intangible property

a. **Grand Larceny** - distinguished from **Petit Larceny** - by the value of the stolen property

4. Property of Another - focuses on possession as distinct from custody or legal title

5. Intent to Deprive Permanently

   a. Specific intent of crime

   b. Prosecution can rely on circumstantial evidence to establish the intent of the defendant

   c. A defendant who takes another's property with the belief that the defendant has a legal right to possession of the property is not guilty of larceny

B. **Embezzlement** - elements:

1. Entrustment of the Property - embezzlers do not "take" property because they already have been entrusted with possession of the property

2. **Conversion** with Intent to Deprive Permanently - use of another's property in a way that is inconsistent with the other's right of possession

C. **False Pretenses** - elements:

1. False Representation of Fact

   a. Can be written, oral or presented in the form of misleading conduct

   b. Must relate to an existing fact, not opinion or promises to do something in the future

2. Knowledge that the Represented Fact is False - actual subjective knowledge that the statement is false - some jurisdictions punish those who assert facts with a reckless disregard for the truth

3. Intent to Defraud the Victim

4. Causing Victims to Pass Title to Their Property - the false representation must have induced the victim to part with the title to property

D. **Receiving Stolen Property** - elements:

1. Receipt of Stolen Property

a. Includes property acquired by larceny, embezzlement, false pretenses, or any other form of theft

b. May be by actual or constructive possession

2. Knowledge that the Property is Stolen

a. Some jurisdictions include recklessness or negligence

b. Defendant's knowledge may be established by circumstantial evidence

i. Purchasing property for a fraction of its real value

ii. Failure to explain possession of recently stolen property

3. Intent to Deprive the Owner of the Property - it is not a requirement that defendant benefit from receiving the stolen property

4. Consolidation of Theft Offenses

a. Some jurisdictions have replaced the common law crimes with a single offense called theft

b. Consolidation statutes usually address aggravated forms of theft

II. Crimes Against Habitation

A. **Burglary** - common law elements:

1. Breaking and Entering

a. **Breaking** - setting aside some portion of the structure that would prevent intrusion

b. **Entry** - an intrusion by any portion of the burglar's body or an instrumentality for purposes of consummating a felony within the dwelling

2. Another's Dwelling

    a. **Dwelling** - a structure in which people normally slept at night

    b. **Curtilage** - the area within which lie structures closely associated with the dwelling

3. At Night - the period between sunset and sunrise when not enough natural light was present to allow discernment of the countenance of a person's face

4. Intent to Commit a Felony Inside

    a. Prosecution may rely on circumstantial evidence to prove the defendant's intent

    b. Does not require that the burglar succeed in consummating an intended felony

B. **Arson** - at common law, the malicious burning of another's dwelling house

1. Mental state: malice, including a specific intent to burn a dwelling or wanton or willful disregard for the likelihood that a dwelling will be burned

2. Dwelling had to sustain damage greater than being scorched by nearby heat or discolored by smoke

3. An explosion that destroyed a building was not arson unless some of the remaining building was subsequently burned by a fire caused by the explosion

KEY TERMS

Arson
Asportation
Breaking
Burglary
Conversion
Curtilage
Custody
Dominion
Dwelling
Embezzlement
Entry
False Pretenses
Grand Larceny
Larceny
Possession
Receiving Stolen Property
Trespass

REVIEW QUESTIONS

Fill-in-the-Blank

1. ______________________, which is an element of common law larceny, is any physical movement of property taken from another's possession.

2. The use of another's property in a way that is inconsistent with the other's right of possession is called ______________________.

3. ______________________ is when a person exercises control over property that has been stolen with knowledge of its stolen nature and with the intent to deprive the owner of the property.

4. ______________________, an element of burglary, is the setting aside some portion of the structure that would prevent intrusion.

5. The area within which lie structures closely associated with the dwelling is called ______________________.

6. ______________________ is the malicious burning of another's dwelling house.

7. The physical control of property is called ______________________.

8. Taking possession of another's personal property without consent or legal justification is ______________________.

Essay

1. Discuss the elements of the crime of embezzlement.

2. Explain the difference between the crime of false pretenses and the crimes of larceny and embezzlement.

3. Discuss the facts a court might consider to determine whether one intended to commit a felony once inside a dwelling, to constitute the crime of burglary.

4. Discuss the elements of common law burglary.

CHAPTER 7

CRIMES AGAINST PUBLIC ORDER AND PUBLIC MORALITY

Crimes against public order and public morality are often difficult to describe and sometimes difficult to enforce. These crimes are often referred to as "victimless crimes," and injure emotional security, morality and the public peace.

This category of crimes is also often controversial. How far does the public want the government to go in defining and policing our morals? How do we decide what activities are moral or immoral? These are some of the questions that will be discussed in this chapter which focuses on the substantive crimes which are considered crimes against the public.

OUTLINE

I. **Disorderly Conduct** - breach of the peace; common nuisance acts that disturb the tranquility or order of the community

   A. **Fighting Words** - words that:

      1. Inflict injury

      2. End to create a breach of the peace

      3. Are not primarily an expression of ideas protected by free speech

   B. **Communication of a Threat** - words conveying the intent to inflict harm; unlike the crime of assault, it does not require a menacing gesture

   C. Indecent or Obscene Words may constitute disorderly conduct if they offend public sensibilities

II. Unlawful Assembly and Riot

   A. **Unlawful Assembly** - a gathering of a designated number of persons (three at common law) for any unlawful purpose or under circumstances endangering the public peace

B. **Riot** - at least one member of an unlawful assembly threatens or commits an act of violence

III. **Public Intoxication** - presence in a public place in a drunken state, which may be a form of disorderly conduct or covered by a specific statute

A. **Driving Under the Influence (DUI) or Driving While Intoxicated (DWI)** - the illegal operation of a motor vehicle while under the influence of alcohol or other drugs

1. **Field Sobriety Tests** - physical coordination or mental clarity tasks administered by a police officer to determine whether a person is drunk; includes such tests as touching finger to nose or walking a straight line

2. **Implied Consent Laws** - possession of a driver's license mandates voluntary submission to blood, breath, or urine tests; refusal to submit results in a suspension of the defendant's driver's license

3. **Habitual Offender** - a person who has been adjudged guilty of drunk driving on a specified number (more than one) occasions

B. Drug Crimes - all states address the supply side by prohibiting the manufacture or actual sale of controlled substances, and most states focus on the demand side by addressing the crimes of:

1. **Actual Possession of an Illegal Drug** - physical contact with or control over the drug, and a mens rea of knowing that the substance is an illegal drug

2. **Constructive Possession of an Illegal Drug** - occurs when a controlled substance is in a place accessible to the defendant and subject to the defendant's control

3. **Possession with Intent to Distribute** - a purposeful plan to sell or provide drugs within the defendant's control to others

4. **Accommodation Defense** - the defendant intended to provide the illegal drug to others without making a profit

C. Nonviolent Sex Offenses

1. **Incest** - sex between closely related family members

2. **Sodomy** - a crime against nature; any sexual intercourse held to be abnormal, especially bestiality or anal intercourse

KEY TERMS

Police Power
Disorderly Conduct
Breach of the Peace
Common Nuisance
Fighting Words
Communication of a Threat
Unlawful Assembly
Riot
Public Intoxication
DUI, DWI
Field Sobriety Tests
Implied Consent Laws
Habitual Offenders
Actual Possession of an Illegal Drug
Constructive Possession of an Illegal Drug
Possession with Intent to Distribute
Accommodation Defense
Incest
Sodomy

REVIEW QUESTIONS

Fill-in-the-Blank

1. Playing a stereo very, very loudly with your windows open would be an example of ______________________.

2. A gathering of a certain number of people for any unlawful purpose or under circumstances which endanger the public peace is called ______________________.

3. ______________________ are physical coordination or mental clarity tasks administered by a police officer to determine whether a person is drunk.

4. A person who has been adjudged guilty of drunk driving on more than one occasion is called a(n) ______________________.

5. ______________________ is a purposeful plan to sell or provide drugs within the defendant's control to others.

6. If A provides illegal drugs to B without making a profit, it is called a(n) ______________________.

7. Sex between closely related family members is called ______________________.

8. ______________________________ are words that inflict injury, tend to create a breach of the peace, and are not primarily an expression of ideas protected by free speech.

Essay

1. Why do some people believe that those who commit "victimless crimes" should not be punished?

2. Explain when indecent or obscene words may constitute disorderly conduct.

3. Explain what implied consent laws are. Do you agree with these laws?

4. Explain what constructive possession of an illegal drug is.

CHAPTER 8

INTRODUCTION TO PROCEDURE AND THE RIGHT TO COUNSEL

Criminal procedure serves two purposes in our criminal justice system. These purposes are identified by the Crime Control Model and the Due Process Model. Both of these models are discussed in this chapter, along with other rights granted by the United States Constitution.

This chapter also explores the constitutional right to counsel and the protection of privileged communication between an attorney and client.

OUTLINE

I. The Purpose of Procedure

A. **Crime Control Model** - focuses on determining factual guilt or innocence; favors only those procedures that help insure the accuracy of the fact-finding process

1. **Factual Guilt** - a showing that in all probability the defendant committed the alleged crime

2. **Legal Guilt** - a factual determination of guilt made in a procedurally correct fashion

B. **Due Process Model** - recognizes that determination of factual guilt may be subordinated to other goals, such as controlling and correcting misconduct by government officials

II. Sources of Procedural Law

A. The primary sources of federal law are the provisions of the Bill of Rights applicable to the states through the Due Process Clause of the Fourteenth Amendment - establish the minimum individual rights which must be recognized by all states

B. States cannot reduce individual rights below the federal constitutional level, but can adopt procedures that create additional rights

C. Each state has procedural rules that govern the operation of its criminal justice system

III. Stages of a Criminal Prosecution

A. **Investigatory Stage** - includes temporary detentions, arrests, searches and seizures, interrogation, and identification procedures as conducted by law enforcement officials

1. Arrests and Temporary Detentions

2. Search and Seizure and Identification Procedures

3. Eavesdropping

4. Interrogation and Self-Incrimination

B. **Adjudicatory Stage** - formal judicial proceedings such as bail hearings, pretrial hearings, and the trial itself

1. First appearance before a judicial officer (bail)

2. Preliminary hearing

3. Charging process (grand jury indictment, information)

4. Pretrial motions

5. Entry of plea

6. Trial

7. Verdict

8. Sentence

9. Judicial review (appeal and habeas corpus)

IV. The Right to Counsel - Sixth Amendment

A. The Right to Counsel at Critical Stages

1. **Adversary Judicial Proceedings** - signal that the government has committed itself to prosecution of the defendant and that the adverse positions of government and defendant have solidified

a. Includes a criminal trial in which the defendant faces a possible sentence of incarceration - applies to both misdemeanors and felonies

b. Applies to pretrial proceedings because the defendant might be prejudiced by the absence of an attorney - depends on whether the proceedings occur after the commencement of the adversarial judicial process

B. Indigents' Right to Counsel

1. **Indigent** - an accused facing prosecution who lacks funds to employ a defense attorney - must be informed of their right to have an attorney appointed at public expense when they face possible imprisonment upon conviction

C. Waiver of Counsel and the Right of Self-Representation

1. Waiver of counsel must be made knowingly and intelligently, usually by executing a waiver in written form

2. Does not permit representation by a third-party non-attorney

3. **Proceed Pro Se** - a criminal defendant waives counsel and chooses self-representation

a. Standby Counsel - appointed by the trial court to aid an accused who later desires assistance in conducting a defense

D. Withdrawal of Counsel

1. Appointed counsel must continue to represent the defendant until replaced by other counsel

2. The defendant or the attorney may request that counsel be relieved for good cause

3. Accused has a right to competent counsel, but no right to representation by a particular attorney

4. Appointed counsel must continue to represent the defendant through any appeals from the trial court

E. Effective Assistance of Counsel

1. Guarantees the defendant reasonable opportunity to consult with counsel before and during trial

2. Defendant must meet two requirements in order to prevail upon a claim of ineffective assistance of counsel

   a. Defendant has the burden to show that counsel's performance was deficient

   b. Defendant must show that the deficient performance prejudiced the defense

F. Representation of Multiple Clients

1. Simultaneous representation of two or more defendants by a single attorney is not a per se violation of accused's right to effective assistance of counsel

2. **Conflict of Interests** - occurs when representation of one client jeopardizes the adequate representation of another; may prevent a single attorney from representing multiple clients

3. An attorney who represents two or more defendants is ethically required to disclose to those clients the possibility of a conflict of interest

G. Attorney-Client Communications

1. **Privilege for Attorney-Client Communications** - protects the confidentiality of counsel's discussions with a defendant

2. The privilege does not extend to communications that enable the client to commit a crime or an act of fraud in destroying evidence or intimidating prospective witnesses

H. Contract to Retain Counsel

1. If defendant is unable to pay the attorney, counsel must decline to accept the case, lower the fee, or advise the defendant to contact another attorney

2. If someone other than the defendant provides payment for retaining counsel, attorney must establish clearly that the duty and loyalty of counsel is to the defendant, not to the person paying counsel's fees

KEY TERMS

Adjudicatory Stage
Adversary Judicial Proceedings
Conflict of Interests
Crime Control Model
Due Process Model
Factual Guilt
Indigent
Ineffective Assistance of Counsel
Investigatory Process
Legal Guilt
Proceed pro se
Privilege for Attorney-Client Communications

REVIEW QUESTIONS

Fill-in-the-Blank

1. The Bill of Rights is applicable to the states through the ______________________ Amendment to the U.S. Constitution.

2. The ______________________ stage of criminal prosecution includes temporary detentions, arrests, searches and seizures, interrogation and identification procedures conducted by law enforcement officials.

3. Formal judicial proceedings such as bail hearings, pretrial hearings and the trial itself are conducted during the ______________________ stage.

4. A(n) ______________________ is an accused facing prosecution who lacks funds to employ a defense attorney.

5. When criminal defendants waive counsel and choose to represent themselves, they ______________________.

6. ________________________ occurs when an attorney's representation of one client jeopardizes his or her adequate representation of another client.

7. ________________________ signal that the government has committed itself to prosecution of the defendant.

8. Confidentiality of an attorney's discussions with a defendant are protected by ________________________.

Essay

1. Explain the difference between the Crime Control Model and the Due Process Model.

2. Discuss the two requirements a defendant must meet in order to prevail on a claim of ineffective assistance of counsel.

3. What must an attorney do if he or she represents two or more defendants? What problems might this attorney incur by this dual representation?

4. Explain the difference between factual guilt and legal guilt. Give an example of each in a particular fact situation.

CHAPTER 9

SEIZURES OF A PERSON AND IDENTIFICATION PROCEDURES

This chapter discusses the procedures that are followed when a person is arrested. It also covers arrests that are made with a warrant and when an arrest can be made without a warrant. The chapter ends with a discussion of the various procedures that are used for identification purposes.

OUTLINE

I. Arrests

A. **Booking Process** - the primarily clerical function of recording information relating to the arrestee's identity

1. Completing the arrest report and preparing the arrestee's permanent police record

2. Fingerprinting and photographing the accused

3. Entering on the police "blotter" the name of the arrestee, the personal effects found in the arrestee's possession, and the date, time, and place of arrest

B. **Summons** - commands the accused to appear at a stated time and place before a court of appropriate jurisdiction

C. Arrest Warrants

1. May be issued by a judge, magistrate, or in some jurisdictions, a clerk of court

2. Must be based upon **probable cause** - a reasonable belief that the suspect has committed a crime

3. **Complaint** - sworn statement of facts establishing probable cause that a person committed a crime

D. Warrantless Arrests

1. Warrantless Arrests in Public

a. **Warrantless Felony Arrest** - taking a suspected felon into custody, which may take place in a public place even though the police had adequate opportunity to procure an arrest warrant

b. **Misdemeanor Committed in the Arresting Officer's Presence** - the officer has direct personal knowledge, through sight, hearing, or other senses, that a misdemeanor is then and there being committed

2. Warrantless Arrests in a Dwelling

a. **Arrest in a Suspect's Dwelling** - taking a suspect into custody that requires either an arrest warrant or exigent circumstances that permit a warrantless entry

b. Exigent circumstances include:

i. Danger to police officers or others

ii. The officer's reasonable belief that contraband is about to be destroyed or removed from the dwelling

iii. Information that the possessors of contraband are aware that the police may be on their trail

iv. The likelihood of escape if the suspects are not swiftly apprehended

3. Consequences of an Illegal Arrest

a. Fourth Amendment exclusionary rule prohibits the introduction of **derivative evidence** - evidentiary items obtained as a result of an illegal arrest

b. Types of evidence that may be suppressed include

i. Tangible items seized during the arrest

ii. Physical evidence such as fingerprints taken from the arrestee

iii. Confessions obtained from the arrestee

iv. Eyewitness identifications contaminated by the illegal arrest

E. **Temporary Detentions** - the suspect is briefly detained, at which time an officer may pat down the suspect's clothing to determine whether the suspect possesses a weapon

1. **Reasonable Suspicion** - the required basis for a temporary detention; the suspect has committed or is committing a crime

2. Definition of a Temporary Detention

a. **Seizure of a Person** - a laying on of hands or application of physical force to restrain movement; or submission to an assertion of authority

b. **Street Encounters** - a citizen is not seized if the totality of the circumstances would lead a reasonable person to conclude that he or she is free to leave

3. Grounds for a Detention

a. Reasonable suspicion for a temporary detention is a lesser standard than the requirement of probable cause for an arrest

b. Reasonable suspicion must be based on specific, objective facts

4. Grounds for Investigation

a. Police officers may frisk or pat down the suspect in order to discover weapons that might be used to harm the officer or others

b. Police officer must have a reasonable basis for concluding the detainee is armed and dangerous

5. Scope of the Investigation

   a. A frisk of suspect may not be initiated for the purpose of seizing evidence, only to discover weapons

   b. "Plain feel" doctrine - officer may intrude beneath the surface of a suspect's clothing only if the officer feels a hard object which could be a weapon, or if the officer recognizes the object as seizable evidence

   c. **Protective Sweep** - a cursory and limited search for weapons within the area under a suspect's immediate control

F. Identification Procedures

1. Lineups and Showups

   a. **Lineup** - a suspect is exhibited to a witness in the company of others similar in appearance to the suspect

   b. **Photographic Array** - photographs of several potential suspects are shown to a witness

   c. **Showup** - a single suspect is exhibited to a witness

   d. **Photographic Showup** - a picture of a single suspect is shown to a witness

2. Due Process and Impermissible Suggestiveness

   a. **Impermissibly Suggestive** - a situation in which the identification procedure gives rise to a substantial likelihood of irreparable misidentification

3. Right to Counsel at Lineups

   a. *Wade-Gilbert* Rule - allows a defendant to invoke the right to counsel as a device for preventing suggestive pretrial identification procedures

   b. *United States v. Kirby* - right to counsel does not attach until the commencement of adversary judicial criminal proceedings

c. *United States v. Ash* - a suspect has no right to counsel at photographic arrays or photographic showups

4. Excluding Identification Evidence at Trial

a. Failure to afford defendant the right to counsel or an identification which violates Due Process results in the exclusion of the pretrial identification

b. Scientific Identifications

i. Fingerprint Evidence

ii. DNA Profiles

iii. HLA Blood Tests

KEY TERMS

Arrest in a Suspect's Dwelling
Booking Process
Complaint
Derivative Evidence
Impermissibly Suggestive
Lineup
Misdemeanor Committed in the Arresting Officer's Presence
Photographic Array
Photographic Showup
Probable Cause to Arrest
Protective Sweep
Reasonable Suspicion
Seizure of a Person
Showup
Street Encounters
Summons
Temporary Detention
Warrantless Felony Arrest

REVIEW QUESTIONS

Fill-in-the-Blank

1. _________________________ is the clerical function of recording information relating to an arrestee's identification.

2. A(n) _________________________ commands an accused to appear at a stated time and place before a court of appropriate jurisdiction.

3. Arrest warrants must be based upon ______________________, which is a reasonable belief that the suspect has committed a crime.

4. The required basis for a temporary detention is ______________________.

5. A cursory and limited search for weapons within the area under a suspect's control is called a(n) ______________________.

6. When a suspect is exhibited to a witness in the company of others similar in appearance, this is called a(n) ______________________.

7. When a picture of a single suspect is shown to a witness, it is called a(n) ______________________.

8. The ______________________ Rule allows a defendant to invoke the right to counsel as a device for preventing suggestive pretrial identification procedures.

Essay

1. Discuss when a person can be arrested in public without a warrant.

2. Explain what derivative evidence is and give an example.

3. Discuss two exigent circumstances which permit a warrantless entry to arrest a suspect in his or her dwelling.

4. Discuss the purpose for which a frisk may be initiated.

CHAPTER 10

SEARCH AND SEIZURE OF PROPERTY

This chapter discusses the Fourth Amendment and the protection of privacy. It looks at the procedural requirements that the government must follow if they intrude upon those privacy rights, such as searches. It also looks at the circumstances that may exist for the government to conduct a search without a warrant.

OUTLINE

I. Reasonable Searches and Seizures

  A. Fourth Amendment serves two purposes:

    1. Protects the privacy interests of individual citizens

    2. Regulates police investigatory activities

  B. **Reasonableness Clause** - "the right of the people to be secure in their persons, houses, papers, and effects, against unreasonable searches and seizures"

  C. **Warrant Clause** - "no warrant shall issue, but upon probable cause, supported by oath or affirmation, and particularly describing the place to be searched, and the person or things to be seized"

  D. Definition of a Search

    1. Physical trespass upon the defendant's private property

    2. Seizure of the defendant's tangible property

    3. Trespass and seizure were pursuant to criminal investigation by law enforcement agencies

    4. **Search** - a government official's intrusion upon a defendant's subjective expectation of privacy; and the expectation is one that society is prepared to recognize as reasonable

5. **Open Fields** - not protected by the Fourth Amendment because a person has no reasonable expectation of privacy in areas open to public view

E. Probable Cause for a Search

1. **Probable Cause** - a reasonable belief that seizable items will be found in a particular place at the time that the search is to be conducted; a flexible standard identified by balancing the degree of intrusion upon individual privacy against the importance of the government purpose to be served by the intrusion

2. The Nature and Location of Seizable Items

   a. Contraband

   b. Weapons and instrumentalities used in the commission of crime

   c. Stolen property

   d. Evidence of the commission of crime

3. The Degree of Probability that Seizable Items will be Found

   a. Probable cause requires less than proof beyond a reasonable doubt and more than a bare suspicion

   b. Magistrates use common sense to determine whether a reasonable probability exists that seizable items are located in the place to be searched

4. The Reliability of the Facts Constituting Probable Cause

   a. **Informant** - a person who does not appear before a magistrate, but who provides information for the issuance of a search warrant

      i. Victim, eyewitness, or responsible citizen

      ii. Law enforcement official

      iii. Previously furnished reliable information to the police

iv. Made a declaration against the informant's own penal arrest

v. Statements have been corroborated

b. **Totality of Circumstances** - facts that establish a fair probability that seizable items will be found in a particular place

5. Execution of a Search Warrant

a. The Time Factor - determined by statute or court rule

b. The Manner of Entering the Defendant's Premises

i. **Knock and Notice** - police must announce their presence, identify themselves, and state their purpose (no knock warrants dispense with this requirement)

ii. Exceptions to Knock and Notice requirement:

(1) When announcing their presence would create a danger to the officers' safety

(2) When announcing their presence would allow suspects to escape

(3) When giving notice would be likely to result in the destruction of the evidence sought to be seized

c. The Scope of the Search

i. **Plain View Doctrine** - the police may seize items not specified in a search warrant if they discover such items while conducting a valid search

F. Warrantless Searches

A. **Search Incident to Arrest** - must be substantially contemporaneous with a lawful arrest

1. Search of the Arrestee

2. Search of the Area Under the Control of the Arrestee

B. Automobile Searches - may occur under three rationales:

1. The automobile may be an area under the control of an arrestee

2. An automobile may be searched in emergency situations

3. An impounded automobile may be "inventoried" pursuant to police department regulations

C. Consent Searches

1. **Consensual Search** - the defendant's permission to search must be freely and voluntarily given

2. **Third Party Consent** - permission to search given by one who shares use, access, or control of the defendant's property or premises

D. Searches Under Exigent Circumstances

1. **Exigent Circumstance** - a situation in which a law enforcement officer confronts "an immediate major crisis in the performance of duty which affords neither time nor opportunity to apply to a magistrate"

2. Obtaining a Warrant

3. Destroying the Evidence

4. Likelihood of Destruction

   a. **Freeze the Status Quo** - an act to prevent the destruction of evidence until a warrant can be obtained, which is permitted when the police encounter exigent circumstances

E. Administrative Searches

1. A search is defined as any governmental action, including inspections by administrative agencies, that intrudes upon a legitimate expectation of privacy

KEY TERMS

Consensual Search
Exigent Circumstance
Freeze the Status Quo
Informant
Knock and Notice
Open Fields
Plain View
Probable Cause
Reasonableness Clause
Search
Search Incident to Arrest
Third-Party Consent
Totality of Circumstances
Warrant Clause

REVIEW QUESTIONS

Fill-in-the-Blank

1. The ______________________ Clause deals with "the right of the people to be secure in their persons, houses, papers, and effects, against unreasonable searches and seizures."

2. The ______________________ Clause states, "no warrant shall issue but upon probable cause, supported by oath or affirmation, and particularly describing the place to be searched, and the person or things to be seized."

3. ______________________ are **not** protected by the Fourth Amendment because a person has no reasonable expectation of privacy in these areas.

4. A person who does not appear before a magistrate, but who provides information for the issuance of a search warrant, is called a(n) ______________________.

5. According to ______________________, the police may seize items not specified in a search warrant if they discover such items while conducting a valid search.

6. ______________________ is when permission to search is given by one who shares use, access, or control of the defendant's property or premises.

7. The ____________________________ are facts that establish a fair probability that seizable items will be found in a particular place.

8. To ____________________________ is an act to prevent the destruction of evidence until a warrant can be obtained.

Essay

1. Discuss the two purposes that the Fourth Amendment serves.

2. Explain what probable cause for a search is.

3. Discuss the three exceptions to the "knock and notice" requirement when entering defendant's premises.

4. When can an automobile be searched?

CHAPTER 11

GOVERNMENT MONITORING OF COMMUNICATIONS AND THE FOURTH AMENDMENT EXCLUSIONARY RULE

This chapter studies different methods of government eavesdropping and how these methods interact with the expectation of privacy rationale under the Fourth Amendment.

It is very important that searches be made legally; if they are not, the exclusionary rule prohibits the prosecution from introducing the evidence that was seized.

OUTLINE

I. Government Eavesdropping

A. The expectation of privacy rationale was extended to reach the Fourth Amendment to certain forms of electronic eavesdropping

B. Warrantless Eavesdropping

1. In the absence of electronic devices, the Fourth Amendment does not apply to governmental action that deceives individuals into revealing information

C. Warrantless Electronic Eavesdropping

1. A listener's use of recording or transmitting devices does not bring Fourth Amendment protections into play

2. **Electronic Tracking Devices** - often some form a "beeper" that emits an electronic signal indicating the position of the beeper placed on a moving person or object

3. **Pen Register** - records the numbers dialed on a telephone by monitoring electrical impulses, but does not overhear conversations

D. Court-Ordered Electronic Eavesdropping

1. **Title III of the Omnibus Crime Control and Safe Streets Act** - a regulatory scheme governing wiretapping and eavesdropping

II. The Exclusionary Rule

A. The Purpose of the Exclusionary Rule

1. **Exclusionary Rule** - bars the prosecution from introducing evidence seized in the course of an illegal search

2. Three justifications (according to Mapp):

a. Judicial integrity requires that courts refuse to become accomplices in the willful disobedience of the constitutional prohibition against unreasonable searches and seizures

b. The intimate relationship between the Fourth and Fifth Amendment establishes the constitutional nature of an exclusionary rule

c. Deterrence of unreasonable searches and seizures can only be achieved by denying law enforcement officials the fruits of their illegality

B. Government Participation in Illegal Searches

1. The Fourth Amendment applies to all federal and state officials and is not limited to law enforcement personnel

2. Whether a private party should be deemed an agent of the government for Fourth Amendment purposes turns on the degree of the government's participation in the private party's activities

3. Foreign law enforcement officials are exempt from the restraints of the Fourth Amendment

C. Standing to Invoke the Exclusionary Rule

1. **Standing** - the defendant must be "a victim of the search or seizure"; the defendant's personal right to privacy was violated

D. **Derivative Evidence: "The Fruit of the Poisonous Tree"** - all secondary evidence obtained by the police as the result of an illegal search

1. The exclusionary rule applies to evidence that is the direct result of an illegal search and seizure

2. Evidence is not tainted when the prosecution establishes:

   a. The connection between the illegal search and the tainted evidence has been weakened by the passage of time or the occurrence of intervening circumstances

   b. The evidence was obtained from a source independent of the illegal search

   c. The discovery of the evidence was inevitable

3. Dissipating the Taint

   a. Passage of time between the illegal search and the discovery of secondary evidence may determine causation

   b. Change in circumstances may break the causal connection

4. **Independent Discovery** - the exclusionary rule does not bar evidence obtained by means unrelated to any illegal search

5. **Inevitable Discovery** - the exclusionary rule does not bar evidence that "ultimately or inevitably would have been discovered by lawful means"

E. Collateral Use of Illegally Seized Evidence

1. **Collateral Stages** - proceedings that do not directly relate to the defendant's ultimate guilt or innocence in which the exclusionary rule is normally inapplicable

F. **Good Faith Exception to the Exclusionary Rule** - the prosecution may introduce the results of an illegal search, if the police relied in good faith upon a search warrant

G. Disposition of Seized Property

1. Any property taken from an accused by an unlawful search and seizure will be returned if the accused is lawfully entitled to have possession of such property

2. Stolen property will be returned to the rightful owner

3. Contraband will be destroyed or otherwise disposed of by court order

4. The government may seek forfeiture of property used in criminal activity

KEY TERMS

Collateral Stages
Derivative Evidence (the Fruit of the Poisonous Tree)
Electronic Tracking Devices
Exclusionary Rule
Good Faith Exception
Independent Discovery
Inevitable Discovery
Pen Register
Standing
Title III of the Omnibus Crime Control and Safe Streets Acts

REVIEW QUESTIONS

Fill-in-the-Blank

1. A(n) ______________________ records the numbers dialed on a telephone by monitoring electrical impulses, but it does not overhear conversations.

2. One must have ______________________, or be a victim of the search or seizure, in order to invoke the exclusionary rule.

3. The exclusionary rule does not bar evidence obtained by means unrelated to any illegal search, or by ______________________.

4. The exclusionary rule also does not bar evidence that would have been discovered by lawful means, or ______________________.

5. Proceedings that do not directly relate to the defendant's ultimate guilty or innocence are referred to as ______________________.

6. The prosecution may introduce the results of an illegal search if the police relied in ______________________ upon a search warrant.

7. A form of a "beeper" that emits an electronic signal indicating the position of the beeper placed on a moving person or object is called a(n) ______________________.

8. Title III of the ______________________ Act is a regulatory scheme governing wiretapping and eavesdropping.

<u>Essay</u>

1. Discuss the justifications for the exclusionary rule.

2. What factors dissipate the taint of evidence which was derived from an illegal search?

3. What must the prosecution establish to show that evidence is **not** tainted?

4. How can seized property be disposed of?

CHAPTER 12

INTERROGATION AND SELF-INCRIMINATION

Chapter 12 discusses the Fifth Amendment protection against self-incrimination. It covers confessions and the rights that must be communicated to a suspect, referred to as the *Miranda* decision. This chapter also discusses the Sixth Amendment right to counsel.

OUTLINE

I. Confessions - the Fifth Amendment provides that no one shall be compelled to be witnesses against themselves in criminal proceedings

A. Voluntariness of Confessions

1. **Voluntary Confession** - a statement of guilt, which is "the product of an essentially free and unconstrained choice by its maker"

2. Voluntariness is determined by considering the totality of the circumstances

a. Physical and Psychological Factors - court looks to the individual characteristics of the defendant

i. Intelligence

ii. Education

iii. Prior experience with police

iv. Use of drugs or alcohol prior to interrogation

v. Emotional or mental disability

vi. Whether the suspect was deprived of physical comforts

b. Police Interrogation Tactics - court considers whether the police interrogators used

i. Violence or threats of violence

ii. Trickery and deceit

iii. Psychological pressures

iv. Threats

v. Promises of lenience

vi. Prolonged and intimidating interrogation

vii. **Admissibility of a Confession** - the voluntariness of the statement, determined by the trial judge; the jury determines the weight to be given a confession

3. The Miranda Decision

a. An individual subjected to custodial interrogation must be advised of certain rights

i. The right to remain silent

ii. That any statement made may be used as evidence against him

iii. That he has the right to the presence of an attorney

iv. That if he cannot afford an attorney, one will be appointed prior to any questioning

b. Warnings must be given regardless of the defendant's possible familiarity with constitutional rights

c. Prosecution bears a "heavy burden" to show that defendant knowingly and intelligently waived the right to silence

d. Accused cannot be penalized for exercising the privilege against self-incrimination

e. Any statement obtained in violation of Miranda is not admissible

4. Custody for Purposes of Miranda

a. **Custodial Interrogation** - questioning initiated by law enforcement officers after a person has been taken into custody or otherwise deprived of his freedom of action in any significant way

b. **Custody** - a formal arrest or restraint on freedom of movement associated with a formal arrest

5. Interrogation within the Meaning of Miranda

a. **Interrogation** - express questioning and any words or actions on the part of the police that the police should know are reasonably likely to elicit an incriminating response from the suspect

b. **Booking Question Exception** - police may ask questions that secure the "biographical data necessary to complete booking or pretrial services"

c. **Public Safety Exception** - the police may ask questions "reasonably prompted by a concern for the public safety"

6. Waiver of Miranda Rights

a. **Waiver of the Right to Remain Silent** - a suspect "voluntarily, knowingly and intelligently" gives up the right not to answer law enforcement officers' questions

b. If suspect chooses to remain silent, the decision must be "scrupulously honored"

7. Sixth Amendment Right to Counsel

a. **Commencement of Judicial Proceedings** - triggers the Sixth Amendment right to counsel during interrogation

8. Corroboration of Confessions

   a. **Corroboration Requirement** - the prosecution must produce independent evidence that establishes the trustworthiness of a confession

9. Suppression of Illegally Obtained Confessions

   a. Silence after the Miranda warnings cannot be used to impeach the defendant or to establish the defendant's sanity

   b. Defendant's pre-arrest silence may be used for impeachment

   c. Defendant's silence in the interim between arrest and the giving of Miranda warnings may be used for impeachment

   d. When defendant waives Miranda rights and makes a statement, the defendant can be impeached by cross-examination focusing on the failure to tell the arresting officers the same story now offered at trial

10. Third-Party Confessions

   a. Prosecution offers the confession of an accomplice who inculpates the defendant in the crime

   b. The defendant offers the confession of a person who then admits to committing the crime

II. Self-Incrimination

A. The Privilege Against Self-Incrimination - the Fifth Amendment provides that "no person ... shall be compelled in any criminal case to be a witness against himself"

B. Compulsion - includes pressures directly applied to the individual or more subtle pressures

C. **Incrimination** - the Fifth Amendment privilege against self-incrimination applies when a "real danger" that the testimony will lead to the imposition of criminal sanctions is apparent

D. Testimonial Communications - the privilege against self-incrimination applies only to testimonial communications

E. Invoking the Fifth Amendment Privilege

1. During pretrial depositions or at trial, privilege must be asserted before an incriminating response is made

2. At trial, the accused in a criminal case cannot be compelled to take the witness stand

F. Waivers and Grants of Immunity

1. A defendant in a criminal trial can make a knowing and intelligent partial waiver in order to testify about collateral matters

2. Two forms of immunity that may set aside the privilege against self-incrimination

a. **Transactional Immunity** - prohibits the trial of an individual for any offense about which the individual testifies

b. **Testimonial immunity (use immunity)** - does not prohibit subsequent prosecution, bars the use of compelled testimony or any evidence derived from the testimony

G. Consequences of Asserting the Privilege

1. Prosecution may not comment on defendant's failure to testify at trial

2. Invited error doctrine authorizes the prosecution to comment on the defendant's silence if the defense "opens the door" by raising the issue of the defendant's silence

KEY TERMS

Admissibility of a Confession
Booking Question Exception
Commencement of Judicial Proceedings
Corroboration Requirement
Custodial Interrogation
Incrimination
Interrogation
Public Safety Exception
Testimonial Immunity (Use Immunity)
Transactional Immunity
Voluntary Confession
Waiver of the Right to Remain Silent

REVIEW QUESTIONS

Fill-in-the-Blank

1. A(n) ________________________ is a statement of guilt which is "the product of an essentially free and unconstrained choice by its maker."

2. Questioning initiated by law enforcement officers after a person has been taken into custody or otherwise deprived of freedom of action is called ________________________.

3. ________________________ is a formal arrest or restraint on freedom of movement associated with a formal arrest.

4. The ________________________ exception states that police may ask questions that secure the "biographical data necessary to complete booking or pretrial services."

5. The ________________________ exception states that police may ask questions "reasonably prompted by a concern for the public safety."

6. If a suspect "voluntarily, knowingly and intelligently" gives up the right not to answer questions of law enforcement officers, this is a ________________________.

7. The ________________________ states that the prosecution must produce independent evidence that establishes the trustworthiness of a confession.

8. Express questioning and any words or actions on the part of the police that the police should know are reasonably likely to elicit an incriminating response from a suspect is called ________________________.

Essay

1. Discuss several police interrogation tactics which the courts will consider when determining if a confession was made voluntarily.

2. Explain the rights an individual must be advised of during custodial interrogation as defined in the *Miranda* decision.

3. Discuss the two forms of immunity that may set aside the privilege against self-incrimination.

4. Explain when the prosecution can and cannot comment on defendant's failure to testify.

CHAPTER 13

PRELIMINARY STAGES OF THE PROSECUTION

This chapter focuses on the preliminary stages of the prosecution. It begins with pretrial release and bail and follows through the preliminary hearing and grand jury review. It then looks at perfecting the charge; duplicity, joinder and charging in the alternative; amending the indictment; and the bill of particulars.

OUTLINE

I. Pretrial Release and Bail

A. **First Appearance before a Judicial Officer** - the initial opportunity for a determination of whether to grant the accused pretrial release, and if so, under what conditions

B. **Bail** - money deposited or bond posted as a condition of an accused's pretrial release from custody

C. **Surety** - one who posts bond on behalf of the accused

D. When determining the conditions of pretrial release, a magistrate is required to consider:

1. The nature and circumstances of the offense

2. The weight of the evidence

3. The defendant's financial ability to pay bail

4. The character of the defendant

E. **Recognizance** - the accused's unsecured promise to appear at proceedings leading up to and including trial

F. When determining whether to release a defendant upon recognizance, the magistrate must consider:

1. The nature and circumstances of the offense charged

2. The accused's family ties

3. The accused's employment

4. The accused's financial resources

5. The length of the accused's residence in the community

6. Any record of convictions

7. The accused's record of appearance at court proceedings or of flight to avoid prosecution

8. Any other available information relevant to whether the accused is likely to appear at court proceedings

G. **Bail Reform Legislation** - pretrial release is determined by considering the nature and circumstances of the offense, the weight of the evidence, the defendant's financial ability to pay bail, and the character of the defendant

H. Bail Reform

1. Federal Bail Reform Act of 1966

   a. Focused magistrate's attention on assuring the defendant's appearance at trial

   b. Federal magistrates could not deny bail and confine the accused in order to protect against future criminal conduct by the defendant

2. Federal Bail Reform Act of 1984 - authorized magistrates to consider the extent to which defendant's release will endanger the safety of other persons or the community

I. Violation of Pretrial Release Conditions

1. Penalties

a. Accused may be found to be in contempt of court

b. Statutes may create a separate offense for disobeying the conditions of pretrial release

c. Accused's pretrial release may be revoked or the conditions of release made more severe

d. Any security given or pledged for the defendant's release may be forfeited

i. **Bond Forfeiture Proceeding** - a civil proceeding to determine whether the surety's bond should be forfeited to the court because the accused violated a condition of pretrial release

ii. **Bail Revocation** - a hearing to consider changes to the conditions of the accused's pretrial release

II. Preliminary Hearing

A. **Preliminary Hearing** - a determination of whether sufficient evidence exists to proceed further in the criminal justice process by bringing the defendant to trial

B. **Probable Cause to Bind the Accused Over for Trial** - the level of proof required at a preliminary hearing; often equated with probable cause to arrest

C. **Prima Facie Case** - evidence that could lead to a conviction if the defense does not rebut it at trial

D. Discovery - the process of exchanging information between the prosecution and defense in order to decrease the opportunities for surprise and gamesmanship at trial

E. Future Impeachment of Witnesses - cross-examination at the preliminary hearing may lead the witness to make statements that can later be shown to be inconsistent with testimony offered at the trial

F. Preservation of Testimony - witnesses who testify at a preliminary hearing may be unable to testify at trial due to death, illness, or other factors that make them unavailable on the date of trial

III. Grand Jury Review

A. **Grand Jury** - a panel of citizens who examine the available evidence and determine whether to indict the accused for a criminal offense

1. Right to grand jury indictment in federal prosecutions comes from the Fifth Amendment

2. Supreme Court held that states are not required to abide by the grand jury requirement imposed on federal courts

B. **Information** - a charge drawn up by the prosecutor and not submitted to a grand jury, although it may be screened by a judicial officer at a preliminary hearing

C. Selection of the Grand Jury

1. Court summons a number of persons qualified to serve as grand jurors

2. **Purging the Grand Jury** - the process of narrowing down the number of qualified grand jurors to the number of jurors who will actually serve

3. **Motion to Quash the Indictment** - raises objections to the composition of the grand jury or the form of the indictment

a. Grounds for objecting to composition of grand jury:

i. One or more of the grand jurors failed to meet the statutory qualifications for service

ii. The process for selecting grand jurors violated constitutional standards

D. Scope of Grand Jury Investigations

1. **Indictment** - a written accusation of crime prepared by the prosecutor and submitted to a grand jury

2. **Runaway Grand Jury** - a grand jury that launches its own investigation and returns charges not requested by the prosecutor

3. **Presentment** - an accusation of crime drawn up at the grand jury's initiative

4. **Subpoena Duces Tecum** - a command to a person to produce writings or objects described in the subpoena

E. Witnesses' Rights Before a Grand Jury

1. A subpoena for the person need not comply with the constitutional standards required for the arrest of a suspect

2. Grand jury may question witnesses based on evidence derived from illegal searches and seizures

3. Witnesses may assert the Fifth Amendment privilege against self-incrimination

4. Witnesses have no right to receive *Miranda* warnings

5. Witnesses who refuse to testify without adequate cause may be found in contempt of court

6. Witnesses have no Sixth Amendment right to be represented by counsel

F. Grand Jury Secrecy

1. Grand jury proceedings are conducted in secrecy

2. Five objectives of secrecy requirement:

   a. To prevent the escape of those whose indictment may be contemplated

   b. To insure the utmost freedom to the grand jury in its deliberations, and to prevent persons subject to indictment or their friends from importuning the grand jurors

   c. To prevent subornation of perjury or tampering with the witnesses who may testify before the grand jury and later appear at the trial of those indicted by it

d. To encourage free and untrammeled disclosures by persons who have information with respect to the commission of crimes

e. To protect the innocent accused who is exonerated from disclosure of the fact that he has been under investigation, and from the expense of standing trial where there was no probability of guilt

IV. Perfecting the Charge

A. **Perfecting the Charge** - the charge must plainly and concisely name the accused, describe the offense charged, identify the place where the accused committed the offense, and recite that the accused committed the offense on or about a certain date

B. Identifying the Accused

1. When no true question arises concerning the accused's identity, the trial court may amend the charge to accurately reflect the accused's name

2. When the entire name is wrong, the charge cannot be amended by striking out the wrong name and inserting the name of the person intended

C. Describing the Offense Charged

1. Must be sufficiently stated to give the accused notice of the nature and character of the crime so that the accused can mount an adequate defense

2. The indictment does not have to allege every fact in the chain of circumstances comprising the offense charged, and it does not have to disclose the prosecution's theory of the case

D. Identifying the Place the Offense was Committed - indictment must identify the site of the offense to establish the court's jurisdiction and venue

E. Stating the Time of the Offense

V. Duplicity, Joinder, and Charging in the Alternative

A. **Duplicity** - more than one offense is alleged in a single count of an indictment

B. **Joinder** - multiple offenses may be charged in a single indictment if the offenses are based on the same act or transaction, or on two or more acts or transactions that are connected or constitute parts of a common scheme or plan

C. **Charging in the Alternative** - the indictment contains separate counts charging alternative ways of committing a single offense

VI. Amending the Indictment

A. Indictments may be amended at any time before verdict provided the amendment does not change the nature or character of the offense charged

B. Amendments cannot save an indictment that fails to state an offense

C. Amendments cannot change a misdemeanor to a felony

VII. **Bill of Particulars** - provides more specific information than what is set out in an indictment

KEY TERMS

Bail
Bail Reform Legislation
Bail Revocation
Bill of Particulars
Bond Forfeiture Proceeding
Charging in the Alternative
Duplicity
First Appearance Before a Judicial Officer
Grand Jury
Indictment
Information
Joinder
Motion to Quash the Indictment
Perfecting the Charge
Preliminary Hearing
Presentment
Prima Facie Case
Probable Cause to Bind the Accused Over for Trial
Purging the Grand Jury
Recognizance
Runaway Grand Jury
Subpoena Duces Tecum
Surety

REVIEW QUESTIONS

Fill-in-the-Blank

1. ______________________ is money deposited or bond posted as a condition of an accused's pretrial release from custody.

2. One who posts bond on behalf of the accused is called a(n) ______________________.

3. A determination of whether sufficient evidence exists to proceed further in the criminal justice process by bringing the defendant to trial is made at the ______________________.

4. A(n) ______________________ is a charge drawn up by the prosecutor and not submitted to a grand jury, while a(n) ______________________ is a written accusation of crime prepared by the prosecutor and submitted to a grand jury.

5. A command to a person to produce writings or objects described in a subpoena is called a(n) ______________________.

6. When more than one offense is alleged in a single count of an indictment, this is called ______________________.

7. ______________________ is when multiple offenses are charged in a single indictment, and the offenses are based on the same act or transaction or on two or more acts or transactions that are connected or constitute parts of a common scheme or plan.

8. A(n) ______________________ provides more specific information than what is set out in an indictment.

Essay

1. Explain how the factors a magistrate considers when determining the conditions of pretrial release.

2. Discuss how the Federal Bail Reform Act of 1984 differed from the Federal Bail Reform Act of 1966.

3. Define discovery and discuss why it is used in a criminal case.

4. Discuss the rights that a witness has when appearing before a grand jury.

CHAPTER 14

PRETRIAL MOTIONS

Chapter 14 examines specifically those motions that may be filed before the trial stage. Motions are filed by both the prosecution and the defense to ask the court to take some sort of action. This chapter covers the most common motions dealing with discovery, statutes of limitations, right to a speedy trial, double jeopardy, severance of offenses or parties, and change of venue.

OUTLINE

I. Overview of Pretrial Motions

   A. **Pretrial Motions** - requests made to a court asking the court to take some action such as dismissing a defective indictment or ordering the parties to disclose certain information

II. Discovery

   A. **Pretrial Discovery** - the process of exchanging information between the prosecution and the defense

   B. Scope of Discovery

      1. Most jurisdictions require the government to disclose

         a. All prior statements of the defendant that are in the possession of the prosecution or other government agencies

         b. A copy of the defendant's prior criminal record

         c. Documents and tangible objects the prosecution intends to use at trial

         d. Scientific reports and tests

      2. Most jurisdictions require the defense to inform the prosecution of the defendant's intent to raise certain defenses

3. Defendant is entitled to inspect material only upon a plausible showing that the material might have exculpatory relevance

4. State is not required to preserve all potentially exculpatory evidence for possible discovery by defendants

C. Prosecution's Right to Discovery

1. Most jurisdictions give the prosecution an unconditional right to be notified prior to trial that the defendant intends to raise the defense of insanity

2. Otherwise, the prosecution's right to discovery is contingent upon whether the defense has been granted discovery

III. Statutes of Limitations

A. **Statutes of Limitations** - specify the length of time permitted between the commission of a crime and the initiation of prosecution

B. **Tolling the Statute of Limitation** - the statute ceases to run under certain conditions, most commonly while the accused is fleeing from justice

IV. Speedy Trial

A. A claim that the defendant was denied a speedy trial must be raised before verdict

B. Sixth Amendment right to a speedy trial does not apply to the period before a defendant is indicted, arrested, or otherwise officially accused

C. Factors which are balanced to determine if the right to a speedy trial has been abridged:

1. The length of the delay

2. The reasons for the delay

3. Whether the defendant asserted the right to a speedy trial

4. Prejudice to the defendant

V. Double Jeopardy

A. **Double Jeopardy** - prohibits the retrial of a defendant who has been convicted or acquitted of the same offense at a previous trial; also protects against multiple punishments for the same offense

B. The prohibition against double jeopardy does not apply until a defendant is put to trial before a jury or judge

1. In a jury trial, jeopardy attaches when the jury is impanelled and sworn

2. In a bench trial, jeopardy attaches when the prosecution begins to introduce evidence

C. **Blockburger Test for Double Jeopardy** - determines whether a defendant's conduct constitutes one crime or separate crimes for purposes of punishment; multiple punishment is permitted if each offense requires proof of an element which the other does not

D. Legislative Intent - if the legislature clearly indicates its desire to impose multiple punishments, it is immaterial whether the punishments are based on a single offense or separate offenses (exception to Blockburger test)

E. Separate Transactions - when multiple offenses arise from separate acts (exception to Blockburger test)

F. **Separate Sovereigns** - exception to the prohibition against double jeopardy; different jurisdictions may impose punishment for the same offense

G. **Collateral Estoppel** - bars the prosecution from relitigating an issue of fact previously resolved in the defendant's favor at a prior trial

VI. Severance of Offenses and/or Parties

A. Joinder and Severance of Offenses

1. The trial court may direct that defendant be tried at one time for all offenses then pending against defendant if:

a. The offenses are based on the same act or transaction

b. The offenses are based on two or more acts or transactions that are connected or constitute parts of a common scheme or pl

c. The defendant and the prosecution consent to a trial for all offenses

2. **Joinder of Offenses** - the defendant faces multiple charges at a single trial

3. **Motion to Sever Offenses** - asks the court to schedule separate trials for separate offenses

B. Joinder and Severance of Defendants

1. **Joinder of Defendants** - one trial of two or more defendants who participated in the same act

2. If defendant objects to a joint trial with other defendants, defendant must file a pretrial motion asking the court to sever the defendants and schedule separate trials

3. A motion to sever the trials of the defendants must be made pretrial

VII. Motion to Change Venue

A. **Venue** - the place where the trial is held

1. In the federal system, only the defendant may request a change of venue

2. Some states allow either the defense or the prosecution to request a change of venue

B. Presumption is that a fair trial can be conducted in the locality where the offense occurred, so burden rests upon the party moving for a change of venue to overcome presumption

C. Alternative methods of counteracting extensive publicity

1. Granting a continuance until publicity abates

2. Issuing "gag" orders limiting any further publicity

3. Exercising great care in selecting jurors who have not been exposed to the publicity

4. Sequestering the jurors to shield them from continuing publicity

5. Summoning jurors from another county or city exposed to less publicity surrounding the case

KEY TERMS

Blockburger Test for Double Jeopardy
Collateral Estoppel
Double Jeopardy
Joinder of Defendants
Joinder of Offenses
Motion to Sever Offenses
Pretrial Discovery
Pretrial Motions
Separate Sovereigns
Statutes of Limitations
Tolling the Statute of Limitations
Venue

REVIEW QUESTIONS

Fill-in-the-Blank

1. Requests that are made to a court asking the court to take some action are called ________________________.

2. ________________________ is the process of exchanging information between the prosecution and defense.

3. The ________________________ specifies the length of time permitted between the commission of a crime and the initiation of prosecution.

4. ________________________ prohibits the retrial of a defendant who has been convicted or acquitted of the same offense at a previous trial.

5. ________________________ bars the prosecution from relitigating an issue of fact previously resolved in the defendant's favor at a prior trial.

6. ________________________ is when the defendant faces multiple charges at a single trial.

7. When one trial is held of two or more defendants who participated in the same act, this is called ________________________.

8. The place where a trial is to be held is called the ________________________.

Essay

1. Explain the types of information the government is required to disclose to the prosecution during pretrial discovery.

2. Discuss the factors that are weighed to determine if the right to a speedy trial has been violated.

3. Explain the Blockburger Test for Double Jeopardy.

4. Discuss the situations when the trial court may direct that a defendant may be tried at one time for all offenses then pending against the defendant.

CHAPTER 15

TRIAL

This chapter looks at the criminal trial, beginning with the defendant's right to a fair and public trial and going through arraignment, entry of the plea and plea agreements, and ending with the trial itself. It covers the evidence that is presented during the trial, including the character of the defendant.

OUTLINE

I. Right to a Fair and Public Trial

   A. Defendant has a constitutional right to a trial before a disinterested and impartial judge

   B. **Motion to Recuse** - a request that the judge step down from the case

   C. Defendant may be deprived of a fair trial if the prosecutor engages in misconduct that prejudices the defendant's rights

      1. Factors to determine if defendant suffered prejudice:

         a. The strength of the properly admitted evidence against the defendant

         b. Whether the prosecutor's misconduct was pronounced and persistent, creating a likelihood that the misconduct would mislead the jury

         c. The action taken by the trial court to correct the prosecutor's misconduct

   D. When prejudicial publicity threatens the defendant's right to a fair trial, the judge may consider options:

      1. Sequester the jury to shield them from any outside influence

2. Remind the jurors that they are not to read or view any media coverage of the proceedings

3. Close portions of the proceedings to the public

4. Issue restraining orders (gag orders) limiting media coverage of the proceedings

5. Grant a continuance until the publicity abates

6. Order a change of venue

E. **Public Trial** - a trial open to observation by all members of the public

II. Arraignment

A. **Arraignment** - identifies the defendant as the person named in the indictment, informs the defendant of the charges, and asks the defendant to plead to the charges

B. **Trial in Absentia** - a trial that proceeds without the defendant being present

1. Factors the judge considers when deciding whether to conduct a trial in absentia:

a. The likelihood that the trial could soon take place with the defendant present

b. The difficulty of rescheduling the trial

c. The burden on the prosecution to secure the attendance of witnesses on another date

d. Any factors given to explain the defendant's absence

III. Entry of the Plea and Plea Agreements

A. Accused has three possible responses to how he or she pleads:

1. Guilty

a. Guilty plea waives many important constitutional rights

b. Must be made voluntarily and knowingly

c. Reduces the grounds for appeal to issues of jurisdiction and the voluntariness of the guilty plea

d. ***Alford* plea** - the defendant pleads guilty but proclaims innocence

2. Not Guilty

3. **Nolo Contendere** - a plea by which the defendant does not admit guilt but will not contest the prosecution's case

a. Functionally equivalent to a plea of guilty for purposes of the criminal trial

b. Cannot be used in any collateral civil proceedings

B. Plea Bargaining

1. **Plea Agreements** - the prosecution and defense agree on the defendant's guilt and the sentence to be recommended by the prosecutor or imposed by the court

a. **Recommendation Plea Agreements** - provide for a sentencing recommendation from the prosecution, but are not binding on the judge

b. **Disposition Plea Agreements** - set specific sentences, which are binding if accepted by the trial judge

2. Many jurisdictions require that the plea agreement be presented to the judge in open court

IV. Jury Trial

A. U.S. Constitution guarantees the right to trial by jury for all criminal cases in which the defendant is charged with a "serious" crime (potential imprisonment of more than six months)

B. Trial by jury is waived when defendant pleads guilty

C. If defendant pleads not guilty, can waive a jury trial if waiver is voluntarily and intelligently given

D. Supreme Court set the number of six as the minimum for a constitutional jury trial

1. If a jurisdiction uses a six-person jury, their verdict must be unanimous

2. If a jurisdiction uses a twelve-person jury, the defendant has no federal constitutional right to a unanimous verdict

V. Jury Selection

A. **Voir Dire** - the process in which defense and prosecution examine the panel of prospective jurors and select the jurors who will actually serve at trial

B. **Challenge for Cause** - may be made against any prospective juror who does not stand impartial in the case

C. **Peremptory Challenges** - may be used to strike any potential juror without stating a reason - cannot be based on race or gender considerations

VI. Presentation of Evidence

A. Opening Statements

1. **Opening Statements of Counsel** - alert the jury to what the attorney expects the evidence to be and how that evidence proves the case

2. Prosecution and defense may not inflame the passions of the jury or appeal to jury prejudice

B. Proving Proper Venue

1. **Venue** - the location of the trial

2. Proper venue must be alleged in the indictment, and at trial the prosecution must prove venue by either direct or circumstantial evidence

C. Establishing Jurisdiction over the Accused

1. **Extradition** - one state surrenders custody of a fugitive who is then transported to another state to face pending charges

2. **Detainer** - a request that a penal institution continue to hold a prisoner for the requesting agency or notify the agency when release of the prisoner is imminent

D. Witnesses

1. The Sixth Amendment does not guarantee an accused the right to compel the attendance of any and all witnesses - defendant must show that the testimony sought would be both material and favorable to the defense

2. Witnesses are notified of expected court appearance by a summons or subpoena, issued by the judge, clerk of court, or the prosecutor

3. A subpoena:

a. Is directed to an appropriate official

b. Names the witness to be summoned

c. States the name of the court and the title of the proceeding

d. Commands the witness to appear at the time and place specified in the subpoena

e. States on whose application the subpoena was issued

4. **Competency to Testify** - the witness has the ability to observe the events about which the testimony is offered, remember such events, understand questions propounded and make intelligent answers, and possess a sense of moral responsibility to tell the truth

E. Real and Scientific Evidence

1. **Real Evidence** - physical objects, most often those discovered at the scene of the crime

2. Relevant scientific evidence is admissible if the device, technique or theory upon which the results are based have gained general acceptance in the scientific community

3. Factors which affect the duty to preserve evidence:

   a. The evidence might be expected to play a significant role in the suspect's defense

   b. The exculpatory value of the evidence must be apparent before the evidence is destroyed

   c. The evidence must be of such a nature that the defendant would be unable to obtain comparable evidence by other reasonably available means

F. Objections and Offers of Proof

1. Failure to object promptly to an item of evidence may constitute a waiver of any objection that could have been raised

2. Objection must be made at the time the evidence is offered

3. Grounds for objection must be stated with specificity so that opposing counsel may have an opportunity to remedy any defect and so that the trial judge may understand the precise question to be decided

4. **Proffer of Evidence** - a stipulation or testimony as to what the offered evidence would have been if the trial judge had ruled it admissible

VII. Defendant's Character

A. Character Evidence

1. When defendant chooses to testify, he places his personal character for truth and veracity at issue, subject to impeachment

2. Impeachment - an attempt to discredit the witness' testimony

3. Most jurisdictions allow witnesses to express personal opinions as to the defendant's character, as well as testimony to the defendant's reputation in the community

B. Evidence of Other Crimes

1. Evidence of specific acts of conduct is generally inadmissible to prove the defendant's bad character or to prove commission of the offense charged at the current trial

2. Exceptions:

   a. To prove motive to commit the crime charged

   b. To establish guilty knowledge or negate good faith

   c. To negate the possibility of mistake or accident

   d. To show the conduct and feeling of the accused toward the victim or to establish their prior relations

   e. To prove an opportunity to commit the crime

   f. To prove the accused's modus operandi when committing certain crimes

   g. To demonstrate a common scheme or plan involving multiple crimes

3. **Limiting Instruction** - the trial judge informs the jury that they may consider an item of evidence for only a limited, proper purpose, and not for an improper purpose

C. Motion for Mistrial

1. Most common grounds for mistrial are the introduction of prejudicial evidence, improper comment of counsel during opening or closing argument, and jury misconduct

2. General rule - an error arising from admission of evidence or improper conduct of counsel may be cured by prompt action of the trial court in instructing the jury to disregard the prejudicial material

3. Must be made at the time the objectionable element is injected into the trial

D. Motion for Acquittal

1. Defense can move for a motion for acquittal after the prosecution has rested its case or at the conclusion of all the evidence

2. Proper grounds is that the evidence is insufficient, as a matter of law, to sustain a conviction

KEY TERMS

Alford plea
Arraignment
Challenge for Cause
Competency to Testify
Detainer
Disposition Plea Agreements
Extradition
Limiting Instruction
Motion to Recuse
Nolo Contendere
Opening Statements of Counsel
Peremptory Challenge
Plea Agreements
Proffer of Evidence
Public Trial
Real Evidence
Recommendation Plea Agreements
Trial in Absentia
Venue
Voir Dire

REVIEW QUESTIONS

Fill-in-the-Blank

1. A request that a judge step down from the case is called a ________________________.

2. The ________________________ identifies the defendant as the person named in the indictment, informs the defendant of the charges, and asks the defendant to plead to the charges.

3. A trial that proceeds without the defendant being present is called a(n) ________________________.

4. ________________________ provide for sentencing recommendation from the prosecution, but are not binding on the judge.

5. The process in which defense and prosecution examine the panel of prospective jurors and select jurors who will actually serve at trial is called ________________________.

6. When selecting jurors, ________________________ may be used to strike any potential juror without stating a reason; however, they cannot be based on race or gender considerations.

7. If Pennsylvania surrenders custody of a fugitive who is then transported to California to face pending charges, this is called ________________________.

8. If defense counsel stipulates or offers testimony as to what offered evidence would have been if the trial judge had ruled it admissible, this is called a ________________________.

Essay

1. Discuss the options a judge may consider when prejudicial publicity threatens the defendant's right to a fair trial.

2. Explain the plea of nolo contendere and discuss the consequences and benefits to the defendant who makes this plea.

3. Discuss the factors that affect the duty to preserve evidence.

4. Discuss the exceptions to the rule that evidence of specific acts of conduct is generally inadmissible to prove the defendant's bad character or to prove commission of the offense charged at the current trial.

CHAPTER 16

VERDICT, PUNISHMENT, AND JUDICIAL REVIEW

Chapter 16 discusses the final steps of the trial: the closing arguments and summations. Instructions are then given to the jury and the jury deliberates and reaches a verdict. Finally, sentencing of the defendant takes place. The chapter ends with a discussion of judicial review of the trial stage.

OUTLINE

I. Verdict and Punishment

A. Closing Arguments and Summations

1. **Closing Arguments** - counsel's summations of the evidence and how that evidence points toward conviction or acquittal - focus on:

a. Summation of the evidence

b. Review of reasonable inferences deducible from the evidence

c. Response to argument of opposing counsel

d. Plea for mercy or "justice"

2. Closing arguments begin with the prosecution and are followed by defense counsel, and then followed by the prosecution's rebuttal

B. Instructions to the Jury

1. **Instructions** - the trial judge's explanations of the law applicable to the charged offense and the evidence presented at trial

2. **Jury Nullification** - a jury disregards the judge's instructions and returns an acquittal because it sympathizes with the defendant or disagrees with the law

3. Mandatory Instructions

   a. Defining the essential elements of the offense

   b. Defining the burden of proof

   c. The presumption of innocence

   d. The defendant's failure to testify

   e. Lesser included offenses

   f. Defenses

4. Instructions Proposed by Counsel

   a. Court may direct counsel to submit proposed instructions

   b. ***Allen* Charge** - may be given when a jury informs the judge that they are unable to agree on a verdict

C. Verdicts, Polling the Jury, Impeaching the Verdict

1. Jury verdict must be in writing, signed by the foreman, and returned in open court

2. **Inconsistent Verdicts** - the jury convicts the defendant of some charges while acquitting of charges that appear to be interrelated

3. **Polling the Jury** - inquiring of each juror in open court, "Is this your verdict?" Each juror must reply in the affirmative or negative.

4. Impeaching the Verdict - the Due Process Clause requires that a verdict of guilty be set aside if it might rest on a legally inadequate basis

D. Sentencing

1. Capital Cases

   a. Judge or jury must consider specific aggravating circumstances

b. Judge or jury must also consider any mitigating evidence

i. The defendant's lack of prior criminal activity

ii. The defendant's extreme mental or emotional disturbance at the time of the offense

iii. The defendant's age at the time of the offense

2. Noncapital Cases

a. **Presentence Reports** - prepared statements that inform the sentencing body of the defendant's background and the circumstances of the offense

b. **Allocution** - the defendant's right to speak in her or his own behalf after the factfinder determines guilt but before the judge pronounces sentence

E. Probation or Suspension of Sentence

1. **Probation** - releases the defendant from custody subject to the condition that the defendant behave in an approved manner, and subject to any other specific conditions imposed by the court

F. Resentencing

1. Resentencing by a judge

2. Jury sentencing

3. **Trial de novo** - a new trial, not an appeal of the lower court's conviction

G. Sentencing for Contempt of Court

1. **Civil Contempt** - the court imposes punishment to coerce compliance with an order of the court

2. **Criminal Contempt** - punishment is imposed to preserve the power and vindicate the dignity of the court

3. **Direct Contempt** - the court summarily punishes without conducting a hearing

4. **Indirect (constructive) contempt** - not committed in the presence of the court; a hearing must be held before the imposition of punishment

II. Judicial Review

A. Judicial Review

1. Trials de novo

2. **Motions to Set aside the Verdict** - directed to the trial court and based on the insufficiency of the evidence, error committed during trial, or newly discovered evidence

3. Preserving an Issue for Appeal

a. **Harmless Error** - does not affect the defendant's right to a fair trial, nor does it call into question the accuracy of the finding of guilt

b. Direct Appeal in the State Courts

i. **Notice or Petition of Appeal** - begins the appellate process by informing the parties, the trial judge, and the appellate court that the case is being appealed

ii. **Per Curiam Opinion** - court decision not attributed to an individual judge, but represents the court as a whole

iii. **Concurring Opinion** - written by a judge who agrees with the appellate court's disposition of the case but wishes to address other considerations

iv. **Dissenting Opinion** - written by a judge who disagrees with the appellate court's decision

c. **Habeas Corpus Petition** - not a continuation of the criminal process, but a civil suit brought to challenge the legality of the restraint under which a person is held

d. Nonjudicial Review of Convictions

i. **Pardon or Grand of Clemency** - forgiveness of a conviction granted by an official of the executive branch - normally, the governor at the state level and the president at the federal level

KEY TERMS

Allen Charge
Allocution
Civil Contempt
Closing Arguments
Concurring Opinions
Criminal Contempt
Direct Contempt
Dissenting Opinions
Habeas Corpus Petitions
Harmless Error
Inconsistent Verdicts
Indirect (constructive) Contempt
Instructions
Jury Nullification
Motion to Set Aside the Verdict
Notice or Petition of Appeal
Pardon or Grant of Clemency
Per Curiam Opinion
Polling the Jury
Presentence Reports
Probation
Trial de novo

REVIEW QUESTIONS

Fill-in-the-Blank

1. Counsel's summations of the evidence and how that evidence points toward conviction or acquittal are called ________________________.

2. ________________________ is when a jury disregards the judge's instructions and returns an acquittal because it sympathizes with the defendant or disagrees with the law.

3. If the jury convicts the defendant of some charges while acquitting of charges that appear to be interrelated, these are said to be ________________________.

4. ________________________ is the inquiring of each juror in open court, "Is this your verdict?"

5. The release of the defendant from custody subject to the condition that the defendant behave in an approved manner and subject to any other specific conditions imposed by the court is called ________________________.

6. A(n) ________________________ is a new trial, not an appeal of the lower court's conviction.

7. ________________________ is when the court imposes punishment to coerce compliance with an order of the court.

8. Forgiveness of a conviction granted by an official of the executive branch is called a(n) ________________________.

Essay

1. What instructions **must** be given to the jury.

2. Explain what mitigating evidence is and give an example.

3. Explain what a harmless error is and give an example.

4. Explain what a habeas corpus petition is.

ANSWERS

CHAPTER 1

Fill-in-the-Blank

1. the degree of punishment and the degree of certainty that criminals will be caught, convicted, and punished.
2. Model Penal Code
3. legislative intent
4. administrative regulations
5. unconstitutionally vague
6. proof beyond a reasonable doubt
7. corpus delecti
8. affirmative defenses
9. presumption
10. permissive inference

Essay

1. The purpose of civil law is to compensate and injured victim. The purpose of criminal law is to punish a wrongdoer.

2. With incapacitation or restraint, the wrongdoer cannot commit future crimes General deterrence deters the public from committing crimes. Retribution vindicates a wrong which has been done.

3. Whether the prosecution or defendant has the burden of proof on each legal issue raised; the amount of evidence required to meet the burden; and the verdict to be returned when the burden is not met.

4. Beyond a reasonable doubt is proof that excludes every reasonable hypothesis except guilt. Preponderance of the evidence determines whether more likely than not (more than 50%) the facts support an affirmative defense.

CHAPTER TWO

Fill-in-the-Blank

1. mental state
   physical act
   social harm
2. deliberate bodily movement
   omission

3. solicitation
4. conspiracy
5. specific intent
6. wanton
   willful
7. reasonably prudent person
   reasonably prudent person
8. strict liability

Essay

1. Criminal law encompasses harm to all of society. Civil law encompasses harm to one member of society.

2. No. Peter has an evil thought. People are not punished for thoughts, only conduct. There must be an affirmative act toward the commission of the crime.

3. Negligence is when one fails to act as a reasonably prudent person under the circumstances. Recklessness is a gross deviation from a law-abiding person's conduct.

4. Factual cause means "but for" a person's act, the social harm would not have occurred. Legal cause is the assessment of the social purposes to be served by the criminal law.

CHAPTER THREE

Fill-in-the-Blank

1. perpetrator (principal in the first degree)
2. aider and abettor (principal in the second degree)
3. compounding a felony
4. merger
5. mere preparation
6. probable desistance
7. abandonment
8. Wharton's rule
9. Pinkerton doctrine
10. overt

Essay

1. Factual impossibility is a claim of defense because the defendant's conduct could

not succeed in brining about the intended offense. Legal impossibility is a claim of defense because the defendant's state of mind precludes commission of a recognized crime.

2. Bonnie has committed the crime of solicitation. Clyde has committed no crime.

3. Under the Pinkerton Doctrine, each member of a conspiracy is criminally responsible for any crime committed by another party to the agreement if it was the object of the conspiracy or a natural consequence of the unlawful agreement. Therefore, B would have criminal liability for the clerk's death since his death was a natural consequence of the robbery.

4. It is a more dangerous situation when two or more people unite to commit a crime than one person acting alone.

CHAPTER FOUR

Fill-in-the-Blank

1. duress
2. alibi
3. irresistible impulse
4. law
5. property
6. involuntary intoxication
7. alter-ego
8. retreat

Essay

1. Even if Calley was ordered to kill those people, he was still presumed to know that the order was illegal.

2. The defendant reasonably believed the threat of harm was imminent; the only way to prevent the threatened harm was to violate the law; and the harm that was caused by violating the law was less serious than the harm the defendant sought to avoid.

3. Mistake of fact is a lack of knowledge of a particular piece of information which may be a defense if it negates a material element of the offense. Mistake of law is a lack of knowledge of a particular law which may be a defense if it negates the mens rea required for the crime.

4. The objective approach to entrapment focuses on whether the government's conduct in inducing the crime was beyond judicial toleration. The subjective approach prohibits police officers from instigating criminal acts by people not predisposed to commit the crime.

CHAPTER FIVE

Fill-in-the-Blank

1. malice aforethought
2. premeditation
3. felony-murder
4. offer type of assault
5. malicious wounding
6. rape shield
7. kidnapping
8. robbery

Essay

1. Malice aforethought occurs when the defendant forms an intent to kill, forms an intent to inflict bodily harm on another, displays a wanton or extremely reckless disregard for the risk to human life, or commits a dangerous felony during the commission of which a death results. Malice aforethought is an essential element of murder, but does not exist in manslaughter.

2. Evidence of planning activity, preconceived motives to kill or indicates that the manner of killing negates the likelihood of a sudden decision to kill.

3. Voluntary manslaughter is a killing while in a state of passion which was caused by adequate provocation and without a reasonable time to cool off. Involuntary manslaughter is a killing that results from the defendant's reckless or criminally negligent conduct or the defendant's commission of an unlawful act.

4. The marital rape exception held that a man could not be convicted of raping his wife. This exception came from the theory that a wife has chattel and when she married, she gave continuing consent to sex with her husband.

CHAPTER SIX

Fill-in-the-Blank

1. asportation

2. conversion
3. receiving stolen property
4. breaking
5. curtilage
6. arson
7. custody
8. trespass

Essay

1. First, entrustment of property, and second, conversion of the property with the intent to deprive the owner permanently.

2. False pretenses is a false representation of a fact with the knowledge that the represented fact is false, with the intent to defraud the victim and causing the victim to pass title to their property. larceny is the trespassory taking and carrying away of the personal property of another with thc intent to deprive the owner permanently of the property. Embezzlement is described in one, above. With embezzlement and false pretenses, the victim willingly passes title or possession of the property. With larceny, the victim does not pass title or possession.

3. Circumstantial evidence which indicates defendant planned to commit a felony. Intent to steal can be inferred if there is no other explanation for defendant's presence in the dwelling.

4. Breaking and entering another's dwelling at night with the intent to commit a felony inside.

CHAPTER SEVEN

Fill-in-the-Blank

1. disorderly conduct
2. unlawful assembly
3. field sobriety tests
4. habitual offender
5. possession with intent to distribute
6. accommodation defense
7. incest
8. fighting words

Essay

1. No one is harmed. There is no individual victim of the crime. Also, some do not want the government involved in regulating our morals.

2. Indecent or obscene words may constitute disorderly conduct if they offend the public's sensibilities.

3. Implied consent laws state that possession of a driver's license mandates voluntary submission to blood, urine, or breath tests. If one refuses to submit to these tests, his or her driver's license will be suspended.

4. Constructive possession of an illegal drug occurs when a controlled substance is in a place accessible to the defendant and subject to the defendant's control.

CHAPTER EIGHT

Fill-in-the-Blank

1. [Due Process clause of the] Fourteenth
2. investigatory
3. adjudicatory
4. indigent
5. proceed pro se
6. conflict of interests
7. adversary judicial proceedings
8. attorney-client privilege

Essay

1. The Crime Control Model focuses on determining factual guilt or innocence, while the Due process Model recognizes that determination of factual guilt may be subordinated to other goals.

2. Defendant must firs show that counsel's performance was deficient and then that the deficient performance prejudiced the defense.

3. The attorney must disclose to all of those clients the possibility of a conflict of interest. Representation of one client may jeopardize the adequate representation of another.

4. Factual guilt is a showing that in all probability the defendant committed the alleged crime. Legal guilt is a factual determination of guilt made in a procedurally correct fashion.

CHAPTER NINE

Fill-in-the-Blank

1. booking process
2. summons
3. probable cause
4. reasonable suspicion
5. temporary detention
6. lineup
7. Photographic showup
8. Wade-Gilbert

Essay

1. First, a warrantless felony arrest, when the police take a suspected felon into custody in a public place. Second, when a misdemeanor is committed in the presence of the arresting officer.

2. Derivative evidence is evidentiary items obtained as a result of an illegal arrest.

3. When there is danger to police officers or others; if the officer has a reasonable belief that contraband is about to be destroyed or removed from the dwelling, that there is information that the possessors of contraband are aware that the police may be on their trail; or if there is the likelihood of escape if the suspects are not swiftly apprehended.

4. A frisk of a suspect can only be initiated for the purpose of discovering weapons.

CHAPTER TEN

Fill-in-the-Blank

1. reasonableness
2. warrant
3. Open fields
4. informant
5. the plain view doctrine
6. Consensual search

7. Totality of circumstances
8. Freeze the status quo

Essay

1. The Fourth Amendment protects the privacy interest of individual citizens and it regulates police investigatory activities.

2. Probable cause for a search is a reasonable belief that seizable items will be found in a particular place at the time that the search is to be conducted.

3. First, when announcing their presence would create a danger to the officer's safety. Second, when announcing their presence would allow suspects to escape. Third, when giving notice would be likely to result in the destruction of the evidence sought to be seized.

4. When the automobile may be an area under the control of an arrestee; if there is an emergency situation; or an impounded automobile may be "inventoried" pursuant to police department regulations.

CHAPTER ELEVEN

Fill-in-the-Blank

1. pen register
2. standing
3. independent discovery
4. inevitable discovery
5. collateral stages
6. good faith
7. electronic tracking device
8. Omnibus Crime Control and Safe Streets

Essay

1. First, judicial integrity requires that courts refuse to become accomplices in the willful disobedience of the constitutional prohibition against unreasonable searches and seizures. Second, the relationship between the Fourth and Fifth Amendments establishes the constitutional nature of an exclusionary rule. Third, a deterrence of unreasonable searches and seizures can only be achieved by denying law enforcement officers the fruits of their illegality.

2. The passage of time between the illegal search and the discovery of secondary evidence that may determine causation and the change in circumstances that may break the causal connection.

3. The connection between the illegal search and the tainted evidence has been weakened by the passage of time or intervening circumstances; the evidence was obtained from a source independent of the illegal search; and the discovery of the evidence was inevitable.

4. Seized property can be returned to the accused if lawfully entitled to possession; returned to the rightful owner if stolen; destroyed or disposed of by court order; or the government may seek forfeiture of property use in criminal activity.

CHAPTER TWELVE

Fill-in-the-Blank

1. voluntary confession
2. custodial interrogation
3. Custody
4. booking question
5 public safety exception
6. waiver of the right to remain silent
7. corroboration requirement
8. interrogation

Essay

1. Violence or threats of violence, trickery and deceit, psychological pressures, threats, promises of lenience, and prolonged and intimidating interrogation.

2. The right to remain silent, that any statement may be used as evidence against him, that the has the right to the presence of an attorney and if he cannot afford an attorney one will be appointed prior to any questioning.

3. Transactional immunity prohibit the trial of an individual for any offense about which the individual testifies. Testimonial immunity does not prohibit subsequent prosecution, bars the use of compelled testimony or any evidence derived from the testimony.

4. The prosecution cannot comment on defendant's failure to testify at trial unless the defense opens the door by raising the issue of the defendant's silence.

CHAPTER THIRTEEN

Fill-in-the-Blank

1. Bail
2. Surety
3. preliminary hearing
4. information
   indictment
5. subpoena duces tecum
6. duplicity
7. joinder
8. bill of particulars

Essay

1. The nature and circumstances of the offense, the weight of the evidence, the defendant's financial ability to pay bail, and the character of the defendant.

2. The 1966 Act focused the magistrate's attention on assuring the defendant's appearance at trial and did not allow magistrates to deny bail and confine the accused in order to protect against future criminal conduct by the defendant. The 1984 Act authorized magistrates to consider the extent to which defendant's release will endanger the safety of other persons or the community.

3. Discovery is the process of exchanging information between the prosecution and defense in order to decrease the opportunities for surprise and gamesmanship at trial.

4. The grand jury may question witnesses based on evidence derived from illegal searches and seizures; witnesses may assert the Fifth Amendment privilege against self-incrimination; witnesses have no right to receive *Miranda* warnings; witnesses who refuse to testify without adequate cause may be found in contempt of court; witnesses have no Sixth Amendment right to be represented by counsel.

CHAPTER FOURTEEN

Fill-in-the-Blank

1. pretrial motions
2. Pretrial discovery
3. statutes of limitations
4. Double jeopardy

5. collateral estoppel
6. Joinder of offenses
7. joinder of defendants
8. venue

Essay

1. All proper statements of the defendant that are in the possession of the prosecutor or other government agencies, a copy of the defendant's prior criminal record, documents and tangible objects the prosecution intends to use at trial, and scientific reports and tests.

2. The length of the delay, the reasons for the delay, whether the defendant asserted the right to a speedy trial, and the prejudice to the defendant.

3. This test determines whether a defendant's conduct constitutes one crime or separate crimes for the purposes of punishment. Multiple punishment is permitted if each offense requires proof of an element which the other does not.

4. If the offenses are based on the same act or transaction; if the offenses are based on two or more acts or transactions that are connected or constitute parts of a common scheme or plan, or if the defendant and the prosecution consent to a trial for all offenses.

CHAPTER FIFTEEN

Fill-in-the-Blank

1. motion to recuse
2. arraignment
3. trial in absentia
4. recommendation plea agreements
5. voir dire
6. peremptory challenge
7. extradition
8. proffer of evidence

Essay

1. The judge may sequester the jury to shield them from any outside influence, remind the jurors that they are not to read or view any media coverage of the proceedings, close portions of the proceedings to the public, issue restraining

orders limiting media coverage of the proceedings, grant a continuance until the publicity abates, or order a change of venue.

2. Nolo contendere is a plea by which the defendant does not admit guilt but will not contest the prosecution's case. This plea is functionally equivalent to a plea of guilty for purposes of the criminal trial, but cannot be used in any collateral civil proceedings.

3. The evidence might be expected to play a significant role in the suspect's defense; the exculpatory value of the evidence must be apparent before the evidence is destroyed; the evidence must be of such a nature that the defendant would be unable to obtain comparable evidence by other reasonable available means.

4. To prove motive to commit the crime charged; to establish guilty knowledge or negate good faith; to negate the possibility of mistake or accident; to show the conduct or feeling of the accused toward the victim or to establish their prior relations; to prove an opportunity to commit the crime; to prove the accused's modus operandi when committing certain crimes; to demonstrate a common scheme or plan involving multiple crimes.

CHAPTER SIXTEEN

Fill-in-the-Blank

1. closing arguments
2. jury nullification
3. inconsistent verdicts
4. Polling the jury
5. probation
6. trial de novo
7. Civil contempt
8. pardon (or grant of clemency)

Essay

1. A definition of the essential elements of the offense; a definition of the burden of proof; the presumption of innocence; the defendant's failure to testify; lesser included offenses and defenses.

2. Evidence a judge or jury may consider to determine sentencing in a capital case. Mitigating evidence will lessen the sentence by the judge or jury. Examples are the defendant's lack of prior criminal activity; the defendant's extreme mental or

emotional disturbance at the time of the offense, or the defendant's age at the time of the offense.

3. A harmless error does not affect the defendant's right to a fair trial, nor does it call into question the accuracy of the finding of guilt.

4. A habeas corpus petition is not a continuation of the criminal process, but a civil suit brought to challenge the legality of the restraint under which a person is held.